THE IMMORTAL FEW

THE IMMORTAL FEW

COMMEMORATING THE BATTLE OF BRITAIN
AND THE AIRCRAFT OF THE BATTLE OF BRITAIN MEMORIAL FLIGHT

"Never in the field of human
conflict was so much owed
by so many to so few."

Winston Churchill

First published in Great Britain in 2010

Copyright © Martin Bowman 2010

British Library Cataloguing-in-Publication Data
A CIP record for this title is available from the British Library

ISBN 978 0 85704 069 5

HALSGROVE
Halsgrove House,
Ryelands Industrial Estate,
Bagley Road, Wellington, Somerset TA21 9PZ
Tel: 01823 653777   Fax: 01823 216796
email: sales@halsgrove.com

Part of the Halsgrove group of companies.
Information on all Halsgrove titles is available at: www.halsgrove.com

Printed and bound in China by Toppan Leefung Printing Ltd

CONTENTS

"The Battle of Britain Memorial Flight is not just a collection of iconic aircraft. It is a national statement, and it is a national treasure. A statement because it reminds the world that freedom must be fought for and was those 70 years ago when Great Britain stood alone. And a statement, too, that we do not forget the sacrifice of all those who flew then and throughout World War 2."

FOREWORD

by Air Chief Marshal Sir Michael Graydon GCB CBE

Each year at 30 seconds to 1.30pm on the first Sunday in July at Capel-le-Ferne in Kent, where stands the Battle of Britain Memorial, the Parade Commander's voice brings the parade to attention: 'Slope Arms'.

As the crash of the rifles dies away, there is silence. And then a sound is heard, a sound that causes the hairs on the neck of the hundreds watching to stand on end. The sound grows and at 1.30pm precisely it reaches a crescendo as an aircraft passes over the saluting base, and the parade presents arms.

That aircraft, a Hurricane or Spitfire of the Battle of Britain Memorial Flight will return later to display to the crowd and especially the Battle of Britain Fighter Association veterans, and often it will be accompanied by the Lancaster.

It is hard to describe the emotion of that moment and the displays that follow it; but the thousands that attend air shows and the many other events that the Flight graces during the summer season will know what I mean. Put simply, there is nothing like it in the world.

The Battle of Britain Memorial Flight is not just a collection of iconic aircraft. It is a national statement, and it is a national treasure. A statement because it reminds the world that freedom must be fought for and was those 70 years ago when Great Britain stood alone. And a statement, too, that we do not forget the sacrifice of all those who flew then and throughout World War 2.

A national treasure because that is what the Flight is; a reminder of our engineering genius, our heritage and the skill and dedication of those who keep these unforgettable machines flying. The Battle of Britain Memorial Flight is truly 'The Best of British'.

Michael Graydon

Air Chief Marshal Sir Michael Graydon GCB CBE
President
The Battle of Britain Memorial Trust

"As soon as you were airborne you pumped the undercarriage up and you were flying a dream. You didn't think about turning, you did turn. Oh how can I describe it? It was a sheer dream. It was an incredible aeroplane, and very fast.

Wing Commander Robert 'Bob' Doe, describing the Spitfire.

INTRODUCTION

by Squadron Leader Ian Smith RAF
Commanding Officer Battle of Britain Memorial Flight

Ian Smith joined the RAF in 1983 and has been flying ever since, amassing 6000 hours in the air. 'Smithy' has flown with the BBMF for the past 4 years as a volunteer fighter pilot, pre-selected to take over as OC BBMF at the end of 2009. This system, which will now continue into the future, ensures that each new OC BBMF gains the necessary experience before taking command of the Flight for a three-year tour. The Officer Commanding is responsible for overseeing all the operations, administration and engineering functions on the Flight, and for the overall planning and management of the extensive display programme undertaken by the BBMF every year. He also holds the post of Fighter Leader, responsible for training the BBMF fighter pilots each year and for conducting air tests on the BBMF fighter aircraft.

It is an honour to introduce myself to you as the Officer Commanding, the Battle of Britain Memorial Flight. Every schoolboy's dream is surely to fly a Spitfire? Not only do I have the privilege I am also humbled to be 'steering' the Flight for the next three seasons.

There is no doubting that the aircraft are the stars but if it were not for the engineering and administrative staff on the Flight the hangar doors would never open. They are the unsung heroes and I ask that you remember their significant contribution when you see us in the skies over Great Britain.

We are very well aware that we have been entrusted with the nations' aviation heritage and we will do our utmost to keep these beautiful and priceless machines where they belong: in the air! With the continued unstinting support of the British public that aim is very achievable.

The Flight is grateful for that support and looks forward to displaying for you during the summer of 2010, seventy years on since the greatest air battle in the history of mankind, and beyond.

Squadron Leader Ian Smith
RAF Coningsby 2010

ACKNOWLEDGEMENTS

The author and publisher wish to record their thanks to the following individuals and organisations who helped in the production of this book:

OCs: Squadron Leader Paul Day OBE AFC, Squadron Leader Clive Rowley MBE, Squadron Leader Al Pinner MBE and Squadron Leader Ian Smith.

Also: Group Captain Stuart Atha DSO; Ron Clark DFC; Sergeant Steve Duncan; Dale Featherby; Flight Lieutenant Jack Hawkins RAFR; Lieutenant Mike Leckey; Group Captain Al Lockwood AFC; Frank Mouritz; Flight Lieutenant Antony Parkinson; Flight Group Captain Peter Ruddock; Squadron Leader 'Shiney' Simmons; Flight Lieutenant Ed Straw; Squadron Leader Dave Thomas; Group Captain Patrick Tootal OBE DL; and all other ranks. Particular thanks to Geoff Simpson.

REMEMBERING THE IMMORTAL FEW

by Squadron Leader Al Pinner MBE

OC BBMF 2006-2009

Born in the mid-sixties, the son of a post-war RAF fighter pilot, my first and lasting passion has been fighter aircraft. As such, it was no surprise that I went on to a career in the Royal Air Force which finally led me to fulfil every schoolboy's dream of flying a Spitfire. For seven wonderful years I flew with the Battle of Britain Memorial Flight, commanding it for the last 4.

It has been an utter privilege to be a small part of this unique commemorative unit. Formed originally to remember The Few, then with the arrival of the Lancaster, to include all those brave members of Bomber Command who made the ultimate sacrifice. Nowadays the Flight is seen as a lasting tribute, a living, breathing memorial to all those who have lost their lives in the air serving this great Nation.

I have frequently been asked which aircraft I most like flying, and in common with all those on the BBMF, it is a signal honour to fly any of them. Annually we receive more than 1100 Bids for our participation at a wide range of events across the country, from Air Displays, through Flypasts to Commemorative events. Some would think that displaying these aircraft must be the pinnacle of any pilot's flying experience, but ask any member of the Flight what means the most to them, and the invariable response would be the Commemorative events. Whether this be on the grand scale over London, at an annual gathering of a dwindling handful of veterans on a windswept disused airfield, or as seems to be far too frequent nowadays, the funeral of one of The Few – it is these events that will stay in the heart far longer than the joy of display flying.

Many thousands of people pass through the hallowed doors of the BBMF each year, ranging from Royalty, Heads of State, Chiefs of Air Forces through to the common man. Many millions more get to see them in their element as they travel the length and breadth of the country through the summer months. The sight and sound of these beautiful machines is so powerful and evocative that it stirs up a huge range of emotions; from memories of brothers, parents, grandparents, to justified national pride; and these former mechanical warriors still inspire in young people a desire to fly.

Reading through this superb personal tribute in words and photographs, I am struck by how long Martin has been associated with the Flight and how well he has done to capture so much of our work for posterity. However, it is the compilation of these modern day photographs with the stories of the likes of Frank Mouritz, Ron Clark and Gerald 'Stapme' Stapleton that make this commemorative edition so special in the 70th year since that fierce battle in the skies that saved our Nation. Sadly, I have just heard that Stapme passed away the week this piece is being written (April 2010), leaving The Few even fewer.

In this special 70th anniversary year of the Battle of Britain, it is right and proper that we pay tribute to those that fought so hard against tyranny so that we might be free, and that we remember the debt we owe to so many brave lives snuffed out even before their prime. While human flesh grows frail, the machines of the Memorial Flight can fly indefinitely, providing a vehicle for us to remember and venerate the Immortal Few.

PART ONE

THE BATTLE OF BRITAIN MEMORIAL FLIGHT

"THE FIRST OF THE FEW & THE LAST OF THE MANY"

The Battle of Britain Memorial Flight (BBMF) is one of the world's foremost historic aircraft collections, maintaining in airworthy condition, the Lancaster (one of only two that remain in flyable condition), five Spitfires, two Hurricanes, a C-47 Dakota and two DH Chipmunks.

In the years immediately following World War Two it became traditional for a Spitfire and Hurricane to lead the Victory Day flypast over London. From this event evolved the idea to form an historic collection of flyable aircraft, initially to commemorate the participation by the RAF in the Battle of Britain and later, to commemorate the RAF's involvement in all the campaigns of WWII. Thus in July 1957 the Historic Aircraft Flight was formed at RAF Biggin Hill, Kent, probably the most famous of all the Battle of Britain stations.

The Flight began with three Rolls-Royce Griffon-engined Mk XIX Spitfires (PM631, PS853 and PS915) and Hurricane LF363, believed to be the last 'Hurri' to enter RAF service. PM631 was too late to see operational service in WW2, being built in November 1945 and delivered to the RAF in 1956. On 11 July 1957, in formation with PS853 and PS915, PM631 was flown to Biggin Hill to form, along with Hurricane LF363, the Historic Aircraft Flight.

Initially, PM631 was in normal camouflage before becoming AD-C of 11 Squadron in 1967. A change to DL-E of 91 Squadron at the time of the D-Day landings was made in 1984 and black and white invasion stripes were painted under the wings and on the fuselage. On 6 June 1984 PM631, Hurricane LF363 and the Lancaster flew over the

Normandy beaches to commemorate the 40th anniversary of Operation *Overlord*. In the winter of 1989-90 PM631's markings reverted to 11 Squadron again as a XIV 'C' and named 'MARY', when serving with SEAC in 1945. The aircraft later represented a PR XIX ('S') of 681 Squadron painted in PR blue without the standard SEAC stripes.

PS915 also entered service just too late for WW2, joining 541 Squadron at Benson in June 1945 before moving to the PR Development Unit to take part in tests of new cameras. In September 1957 PS915 was grounded and became a gate guardian for almost 30 years, until in 1986 it returned to the Flight. In 1987 it carried no squadron codes but was finished in the typical PR overall blue colour scheme. Like PS853, PS915 was modified to take a Mk 58 Griffon engine from the Avro Shackleton. PS915 was subsequently painted to represent the Prototype Mk.XIV (JF319).

In October 1957 Mk XVI Spitfires TE330, TE476 and SL674 joined the Flight. In April 1958 Spitfire XIX PS853 left the Flight but rejoined in 1964. It swapped its camouflage scheme for PR blue in 1973-74 but the matt paint was replaced late in 1974 by a gloss finish. For the 1990 season the markings changed to C of 16 Squadron, which operated PS853 during 1945-46 as part of the 2nd Tactical Air Force (2nd TAF).

During the period February to May 1958 Biggin Hill closed and the Flight moved to another famous Battle of Britain station, at RAF North Weald in Essex. When this station closed the Flight moved again, to RAF Martlesham Heath in Suffolk. In 1958 Spitfire XVI TE330 was

This is a famous photograph of 242 Squadron pilots at RAF Coltishall, Norfolk in late September 1940. Standing left to right: Pilot Officer Denis W. Crowley-Milling, who remained with 242 Squadron until the spring of 1941, receiving a DFC on 11 April; Pilot Officer Hugh Tamblyn, a 23-year old ex-Defiant pilot who was decorated with the DFC by HM the King on 1 April 1941. Two days later he was shot down and killed; Pilot Officer 'Stan' Turner; Pilot Officer Norman Neil Campbell of St Thomas, Ontario (KIA 17 October 1940); Squadron Leader Douglas Bader; Flight Lieutenant George Eric Ball; Pilot Officer Michael Giles Homer DFC (KIA 27 September 1940), and Pilot Officer Marvin Kitchener 'Ben' Brown (killed on a local flight on 21 February 1941). Ball received a bar to his DFC on 1 October 1940. At the end of January 1941 he was posted out to the Middle East, joining 73 Squadron as a flight commander in the Desert. On 12 April he flew into a sandstorm and was forced to land in Axis territory, spending the rest of the war as a PoW. On release in 1945 he joined 567 Squadron, an anti-aircraft co-operation unit, briefly. In October he was promoted Squadron Leader and given command of 222 Squadron on Meteor F.3 jets. He was killed in a flying accident on 1 February 1946, aged 27. Behind Bader's right shoulder is Flight Lieutenant 'Willie' McKnight DFC (KIA 12 January 1941 on a low level 'Rhubarb' operation). Sergeant John Ernest Savill sits on the wing with his left hand on the cockpit sill. Having joined the RAFVR in December 1937 Savill was called up on 1 September 1939. He was with 151 Squadron at Martlesham Heath in July 1940, shooting a Dornier Do 17 down on 13 August. He was posted to 242 Squadron on 21 September, promoted Warrant Officer on 1 October and posted to 501 Squadron on the 12th. Early in 1941 Bader began leading squadrons of Hurricane IIs on offensive sweeps over France from North Weald. In March 1941 he was appointed Wing Commander Flying at Tangmere flying Spitfires on offensive sweeps over the continent. He had been awarded a DFC in January 1941 for ten victories and a bar to his DSO followed in July for 15, and a bar to his DFC came in September, for four more. On 9 August Bader was shot down over France on a fighter sweep and he spent the rest of the war in German prison camps until finally being released from Colditz Castle in April 1945.

donated to the USAF Academy at Colorado Springs. Up until 1959 LF363 was used to lead the annual flypast over London on Battle of Britain Sunday. However, when Spitfire XVI SL574 suffered an engine failure overhead Bromley in Kent during the flypast and the pilot had to make a wheels-up landing on the cricket pitch of the OXO sports ground further participation by the Flight was cancelled and only resumed again in 1986. TE476 and SL674 were powered by Packard built Merlins and as such were considered unsafe for further flight. TE476 became the gate guardian at the famous Battle of Britain fighter

station at RAF Coltishall for a time, while SL574, after it had been repaired, became gate guardian at HQ Fighter Command at Bentley Priory in 1961.

In November 1961 the Flight moved to Norfolk, first to RAF Horsham St Faith (now Norwich Airport) and then on 1 April 1963, to RAF Coltishall, which had been a 12 Group Station in Fighter Command. During the Battle of Britain many famous squadrons and pilots such as Douglas Bader, Robert Stanford Tuck and 'Johnnie' Johnson operated from here. In 1965 the Flight acquired Spitfire Vb

AB910 from Vickers Armstrong (BAC) and on 16 September Jeffrey Quill the company's chief test pilot flew it to RAF Coltishall. Built at Castle Bromwich in August 1941 AB910 saw service with 222 (Natal), 130 (Punjab), and 133 (Eagle) Squadrons. On 19 August 1942, when 133 Squadron at Lympne was ordered to patrol the Dieppe area AB910 flew four sorties. On his second patrol in AB910 Flying Officer Doorly shared in the destruction of two Fw 190s and a Ju 88, while four more Fw 190s and three Do 217s were damaged. On his third patrol that day, Flight Sergeant Richard L. 'Dixie' Alexander, an American from Grant Park, Illinois shot down a Do 217 flying AB910. The aircraft was transferred to 242 (Canadian) Squadron on 2 September 1942 and it later served with 416 ('City of Oshawa') and 402 ('Winnipeg Bear') Squadrons, RCAF. Later, at 53 OTU at Hibaldstow, ACW2 Margaret Horton was inadvertently taken aloft as she gripped the tail of the aircraft! Normally, the 'tail weight' would sit there to the end of the runway but before she had time to dismount, Flight Lieutenant Neil Cox, the pilot began the take off! One circuit later and with the aircraft handling strangely, Cox landed, still with a very frightened WAAF wrapped around the tail.

On 20 August 1978 AB910 had just begun its take off run during an air show at Bex in Switzerland when a Dutch Harvard turned onto the runway in front of the Spitfire and a collision resulted. There was no fire although the Spitfire was badly damaged and it had to be recovered to Abingdon for a major rebuild and then to Kemble for full servicing. AB910 did not fly again until 27 October 1981, when it rejoined the Flight. Early in 1997 AB910 was dismantled and airfreighted across the Atlantic, carrying the markings of 71 (Eagle) Squadron for the USAF celebrations in America before returning to the UK and the planned repainting of the aircraft in 222 (Natal) Squadron colours as ZD-C. During major servicing in winter 2002/03 AB910 was repainted to represent Mk Vb AB502 of No 244 Wing in Tunisia 1943 flown by Wing Commander Ian Richard Gleed DSO DFC.

In October 1968 the Flight acquired Spitfire IIa P7350 after the filming of *The Battle of Britain*. The Flight's Spitfire XIXs and AB910 also took part in the film, as did Hurricanes PZ865 and LF363, which had both featured in *Angels One Five* in 1952. P7350 was now the oldest aircraft on the Flight, having been built at Castle Bromwich in 1940 as the 14th of 11,989 Spitfires, entering service that August and serving on Nos. 266 (Rhodesia), 603 (City of Edinburgh), 616 (South Yorkshire, AAF) and 64 Squadrons in turn. In 1969 and 1972 P7350 was painted to represent 266 (Rhodesia) Squadron and during the winter of 1977-

78 these gave way to QV-B of 19 Squadron which were used until 1981-82 when it became SH-D, a 64 Squadron aircraft. In 1985 P7350 was repainted as EB-Z 'Observer Corps' of 41 Squadron, which was a presentation aircraft, sponsored by the Royal Observer Corps in WW2. In 1988 P7350 was painted in its original 266 Squadron code, UO-T. By 1994 P7350 had also featured as YT-F of 65 (East India) Squadron and Mk IIa P7832 *Enniskillen* of 72 Squadron.

In 1969 LF363 was painted to represent V7467 LE-D of 242 (Canadian) Squadron flown by Squadron Leader Douglas Bader at Coltishall and Duxford in the summer of 1940. Hurricane LF363 was in turn painted to represent Hurricanes of 249 (Gold Coast) Squadron, including, GN-A, the aircraft flown by Flight Lieutenant James Nicholson whose actions on 17 August 1940 earned him the award of the Victoria Cross (the first and only VC awarded to Fighter Command). In January 1983 LF363 was repainted all black and given the codes 'VY-X' to represent a Hurricane night fighter of 85 Squadron, which operated from Debden, Essex during the Battle of Britain.

Meanwhile, Hurricane IIc PZ865, the last of 12,780 Hurricanes to be built in Britain, was acquired from Hawker Aircraft and flown to Coltishall in March 1972 after a complete overhaul. It carried the standard factory-applied camouflage finish and the inscription *The Last of the Many!,* as was applied to the fighter on its roll-out at Langley, Buckinghamshire in 1944. These markings were then reapplied to the Hurricane for the 1982 season.

In July 1972 PZ865 was repainted as Hurricane I V6962 DT-A to represent the aircraft of 257 (Burma) Squadron as flown by the CO, Squadron Leader Robert Stanford Tuck DFC in September 1940. PZ865 then operated in the representative colours of JU-Q of 'Treble One' Squadron and in 1988, as RF-U, one of the aircraft flown by Sergeant Josef František of 303 'Warsaw-Kosciuszko' Squadron in the Battle of Britain. The Polish squadron was formed at RAF Northolt on 22 July 1940 from pilots of the 111 'Kosciuszko' and 112 'Warsaw' Eskadra of the *Lotnictwo Woljskowe* (Polish Air Force) evacuated from France and thus became the second Polish fighter Squadron to form in the RAF. After the defeat of Poland and then France, where Polish fighter pilots distinguished themselves in action against the Luftwaffe, they had joined the British cause in its hour of greatest need. In 1939 František, a Czech, escaped to Poland, machine gunning invading German troop columns converging on Prague as he went, and flew the Polish Air Force PZL in action against the Luftwaffe. He shot down four Bf 109s but the tiny Polish Air Force was heavily outnumbered and he arrived in France in

October, seeing action in 1940 with the *Armée de l'Air*. After the Battle of France František volunteered for the RAF in June 1940 and he became the highest scoring RAF pilot in the Battle of Britain with 17 victories achieved over 11 days in September. On 8 October František was killed returning to Northolt from an early morning patrol when his Hurricane crashed beside a golf course at Ewell, Surrey.

From 1993, PZ865 was flown in the markings of Hurricane I P3731 of 261 Squadron, which was one of the first twelve Hurris to be delivered to Malta aboard the aircraft carrier HMS *Argus* in Operation 'Hurry' in August 1940.

Having also acquired Avro Lancaster B.I PA474 from 44 Squadron, in 1973 the Flight's name changed to Battle of Britain Memorial Flight. With the arrival of Jaguar aircraft at Coltishall the decision was taken to move the BBMF to RAF Coningsby in March 1976 to free up more space on the Norfolk station for the new jets. Such was their popularity that just before the BBMF left Coltishall, more than 7,000 local people gathered for one last look at these historic aircraft that had been honoured and welcome guests in the county for over 15 years.

In April 1983 the Flight acquired Chipmunk T.10 WK518. In 1985 de Havilland DH Devon was acquired and was used by the Flight until retirement in 1993, being sold in 1997. In June 1995 the Flight acquired its second Chipmunk T.10 when WG486, part of the RAF Gatow Station Flight in Berlin, arrived at Coningsby. It became the most unlikely 'spy plane' during the Cold War until the Berlin Wall came down on 9 November 1989. The Chipmunks, which appear in high-conspicuity black paint scheme with white bars, are used year round primarily for the conversion and continuation training of BBMF pilots on tail wheel aircraft.

On 11 September 1991, while en route from Coningsby to Jersey, Hurricane LF363's engine started running rough, pouring smoke from all twelve exhaust stubs, the pilot, Squadron Leader Allan 'Slam' Martin, attempted to land at Wittering, but the engine then failed completely, resulting in a crash-landing on the airfield. Martin suffered some burns and a broken ankle as he scrambled away from the fierce fire, which engulfed the Hurricane. The decision was taken to rebuild the aircraft and restore it to flying condition. On 13 February 1995 Spitfire XIX PS853 was sold and the proceeds used to help fund the cost of rebuild, LF363 returning to service in September 1998. It was painted to represent R4197 US-C of 56 Squadron stationed at North Weald during the Battle of Britain. Appropriately, 56 Squadron's crest features a 'Phoenix rising from the Ashes'! R4197 was shot down on 31 August 1940 after

tangling with an overwhelming number of Bf 110s of ZG26. Pilot Officer Maurice Mounsdon bailed out after suffering severe burns and he subsequently became a member of the 'Guinea Pig Club' for burned airmen. LF363's misfortunes continued during 2004, when on 6 June the starboard undercarriage collapsed on landing at Duxford. Fortunately, the damage was only minor and the aircraft was fully repaired over the winter servicing period.

In July 1993 C-47 (Douglas DC-3 Dakota III ZA947) was acquired. This aircraft was built in March 1942 and was operated by the Royal Canadian Air Force (RCAF). Declared surplus in 1971 the aircraft was purchased by the Royal Aircraft Establishment (RAE) at Farnborough who operated the C-47 until RAF Strike Command adopted the aircraft in March 1993 when it was issued to the BBMF. At RAF Marham the aircraft was painted to represent posthumous VC recipient, Flight Lieutenant David Lord DFC's aircraft (YS-DM), which he flew during the fateful *Market* operation at Arnhem on 19 September 1944. In 1998, during a minor servicing with Air Atlantique at Coventry, ZA947's markings were changed to YS-H of 77 Squadron. In 1948, while stationed at Fassberg in Germany, 77 Squadron took part in the Berlin Airlift.

In January 2003 the Dakota was repainted in the livery of 267 'Pegasus' Squadron, which operated from Bari in Italy in the transport and trooping role in 1943-44. The Squadron employed various colour schemes on its Dakotas but always displayed the 'Pegasus' emblem prominently on the aircraft's nose. The Squadron's role included the re-supply of partisans and resistance fighters, behind enemy lines, either by para-drops or by landing at clandestine airstrips. The BBMF Dakota earns its keep in the training of new aircrew and in keeping the pilots of the Lancaster current during the winter months when the bomber is out of action.

In January 1992 a complete refurbishment to flying condition of Spitfire IX MK356, which had been on display in the museum at St Athan was begun. As the aircraft's mainspars were badly damaged, the clipped wings of a Mk.XVI were substituted. Following the war, the aircraft was used for gate-guardian duties and also appeared as a static airframe in the film *The Battle of Britain* before going to St Athan. The aircraft's first flight for 53 years took place on 7 November 1997. A week later it was flown to its new home at Coningsby to join the BBMF, painted in the only operational markings it ever wore operationally as 21-V of 443 Squadron RCAF complete with black and white D-Day stripes on the underside of the wings and fuselage.

"It had been 'a piece of cake' we said a few hours later, when we happily caught sight of Lincoln Cathedral in the spring sunshine. How many times had I looked down on the majestic 800 year old Norman cathedral, bathed in the amber reflection of an autumn sunset, as we circled before setting course for Germany? And again, shrouded in misty winter dawns as we let down through the clouds on our return."

Peter Bone, Lancaster mid-upper gunner, 626 Squadron, Wickenby

19

PR XIX PS915 spent the winter of 1997 at RAF St Athan on major servicing and reappeared representing a XIV in the markings of 152 (Hyderabad) Squadron of SEAC (UM-G) complete with pouncing black panther motif on the port side of the fuselage. Spitfire IIa P7350 was painted in the markings of 277 Search and Rescue Squadron at Hawkinge, Kent but unfortunately not flown in displays until that September due to the shortage of a Merlin engine. The aircraft represented P8509 BA-Y 'THE OLD LADY', which was given by the Bank of England, affectionately known as 'The Old lady of Threadneedle Street'. Following a major servicing at St Athan over the winter of 1998 Hurricane PZ865 adopted the colours of a 5 Squadron Hurricane IIc and coded 'Q', which were used during the squadron's time in South East Asia Command (SEAC). In the spring of 1999 P7350's markings were changed again to represent L1067 XT-D of 603 'City of Edinburgh' Squadron, Auxiliary Air Force, the aircraft flown by Squadron Leader

George 'Uncle' Denholme DFC during the Battle of Britain. The inscription BLUE PETER refers to a famous Derby winning racehorse. On 30 August 1940, while operating from Hornchurch, L1067 was hit by return fire during a combat with Bf 110s and Denholme was forced to bail out. He survived the war, retiring as a Group Captain. His Spitfire crashed at Hope Farm, Snargate where it was excavated in 1973 and various parts including the fuel tank panel bearing the words BLUE PETER were uncovered.

In the year 2000, the BBMF was granted semi-autonomous status as an independent unit. In April 2002 two non-flying Spitfire XVIs (TE311 and TB382) were allocated to BBMF for spares support. TB382 was dismantled for spares and struck off charge while TE311 became part of a 'spares recovery' programme. PZ865 emerged from a major servicing over the winter of 2004/05 in a new colour scheme representing Hurricane IIC BE581 'NIGHT REAPER, as flown by the Czech fighter ace, Flight Lieutenant Karel Kuttelwascher during night intruder operations from Tangmere in 1942 with No.1(F) Squadron. Spitfire PR XIX PS915 meanwhile, also emerged from a major servicing carried out by the Aircraft Restoration Company at Duxford during the winter of 2003/04 in the colour scheme used by PR XIX PS888 of 81 Squadron at Seletar, Singapore. This aircraft flew the last operational sortie by a RAF Spitfire when, on 1 April 1954, it flew a photographic sortie over an area of jungle in Johore thought to contain hideouts for Communist guerrillas. For the occasion, the inscription, "THE LAST!' was painted on the nose. After a major servicing during the winter of 2005/06, Hurricane IIc LF363 re-appeared in the markings of Hurricane I P3878 YB-W. This was the aircraft of Flying Officer Harold 'Birdy' Bird-Wilson (later Air Vice Marshal Bird-Wilson CBE DSO DFC* AFC*) 17 Squadron during the Battle of Britain.

In 2007 the BBMF celebrated its 50th Anniversary of Commemorative service. Spitfire Vb AB910 emerged from the winter break as EN951 RF-D, the aircraft of Squadron Leader Jan Zumbach, CO, 303 'Kosciuszko' Squadron, while Spitfire PR XIX PM631, which has remained in flying condition with the Flight since its inception, appropriately marked its 50th year of continuous service on display duties.

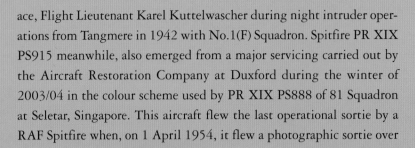

23

"*Spitfires full out, 300 mph. 350, 380, 400 and there was the enemy. I picked mine and attacked. I saw him lurch, a flame from his engine, which went out, and then I saw his tracer bullets coming back at me and I broke away like mad. By this time George who had lost his in clouds joined me and we started to beat him up together. The Hun trying to dodge into the clouds all the time, but one of us always headed him off. At last the poor devil crashed into the water. As there was a destroyer near, I circled round them for a little. The pilot was saved, but all the other three had been shot dead. P.S. There is a lovely line in today's* Scottish Express *about a sheep farmer (sic) and a plasterer shooting down a Hun.*"

Squadron Leader Archie McKellar DSO DFC* 602 Squadron Spitfire I pilot, 16 October 1939 when he and 30-year old Flight Lieutenant George Pinkerton were awarded half-shares in the destruction of a Ju 88A-1. As a boy McKellar had two ambitions – to become a plasterer and to fly. Born at Paisley in 1912 he was the only child of John McKellar who had served his apprenticeship as a plasterer before launching into business as a contractor. Pinkerton was a fruit farmer in Renfrewshire where his wife and 6-month-old daughter lived.

24

Since its formation in 1957, the aircrew on the Flight have been drawn from volunteers, all of whom perform their primary duties on front-line types such as the Eurofighter Typhoon II and the Boeing E-3D AWACs or on training aircraft such as the Beech Super King Air. The one exception is the Officer Commanding, for whom the demands of overseeing operations including display-related planning, administration and engineering means that he serves full-time with the BBMF. The OC is assisted by a retired officer as the Flight's Operations Officer/Adjutant, a Public Relations Officer, an Operations Assistant and a civilian Administrative Assistant. In the early years engineers, like the aircrew, made themselves available largely on a voluntary, self-help basis, though of course they were fully qualified in the various aspects of the aircraft. With the expansion of

Navarone. PA474 was to have been put on permanent display at RAF Hendon but fortunately a decision was taken to return the bomber to flying condition. The aircraft eventually joined the Flight in November 1973 and it wore the markings of the Lancaster (KM-B) flown by Squadron Leader John Nettleton of 44 Squadron who was awarded the Victoria Cross for his heroism on the Augsburg raid, 17 April 1942. Following the 1979 season the Lancaster was repainted as ED932 AJ-G of 617 Squadron flown by Wing Commander Guy Gibson DSO* DFC* on the Ruhr dams' raid of 16/17 May 1943.

PA474's next scheme, in 1984, was as SR-D of 101 Squadron, followed in 1988 as PM-M² - better known as *Mike Squared,* which served with 103 and 576 Squadrons and completed 140 operational

the fleet in the mid-1970s, engineering was placed on a more formal basis and the team now consists of 25 full-time ground crew personnel led by a Warrant Officer Engineering Officer. Throughout the season these personnel maintain the BBMF's fleet of historic aircraft at RAF Coningsby and off station on the display circuit.

British industry normally carries out all major (deep-strip) servicing and the opportunity is taken to change the historic aircraft's warpaint. The fighters have appeared in the livery of several famous squadrons and the Lancaster often acquires a new winter coat. There have been 36 Lancs that famously recorded 100 or more wartime operations and all but one of them was unceremoniously reduced to scrap after the end of hostilities so PA474 has represented several centenarians after more 'humble' beginnings. In 1964 PA474 was painted in a camouflage scheme, though without squadron markings. During this period the Lanc took part in two major feature films - *Operation Crossbow* and *The Guns of*

sorties, a Bomber Command record. In May 1974 PA474 was christened *City of Lincoln* and city's coat of arms was proudly displayed to the left hand side of aircraft just forward of the cockpit in recognition of the county's strong association with the Lancaster and Bomber Command. At a ceremony at Waddington on 8 May 1975, shortly before the BBMF moved to Coningsby, the City of Lincoln formally adopted PA474. In 1993-94 the size of the nose art of *Still Going Strong!* (better known as *Johnnie Walker*) applied to the left hand side of the aircraft resulted in the name and coat of arms having to be moved to the right hand side of the aircraft, where it has remained ever since. W4964 WS-J of 9 Squadron flew its 100th operation on 15 September 1944 when Nos. 9 and 617 'Dam Busters' Squadrons carried out the first attack on the *Tirpitz* from Russia. After dropping its 12,000lb TALLBOY bomb, Flight Lieutenant Doug Melrose and his crew returned to Bardney to receive a well-earned crate of whiskey.

PA474 has often flown over several of the lakes such as Uppingham (Rutland Water), Abberton near Colchester and Derwent Water (Ladybower Reservoir) which the 'Dam Busters' practiced on before the famous Ruhr dams' raid. (Although the dam on the Ladybower Reservoir was completed in 1943 it did not actually hold any water when 617 Squadron were training). On Wednesday 19 May 1993, on the 50th Anniversary Commemoration of Operation CHASTISE, PA474 memorably crested the parapet of the Derwent Dam and flew between its twin towers. Present were former Dam Buster pilots, Les Munro and Joe McCarthy and Richard Todd, star of the famous 1954 film, and several thousand spectators packed into the length and breadth of the Derwent Valley.

From 2000 to 2 October 2006 PA474 flew in the markings and livery of Lancaster III EE176 QR-M MICKEY THE MOOCHER of 61 Squadron stationed at Skellingthorpe. In 2007 the BBMF Lancaster emerged as 'PHANTOM OF THE RUHR'.

For many years after its formation the Flight conducted relatively low-key operations; typically making 50-60 appearances per season. This situation continued into the mid-1960s and by 1992 participation was up to 150 appearances, growing to 200 in 1995 and exceeding 500 in 1996. Since 2003 the Flight has been tasked for over 700 individual aircraft appearances during each year's display season and this is now considered the norm.

Transit flights between displays and flypasts provide exciting opportunities for photographing the Lancaster and the BBMF fighters passing Lincoln and Ely cathedrals, the 'Boston Stump' and cities like Norwich, which every September enjoys a special Battle of Britain flypast in recognition of the time the Flight spent in Norfolk. Lincoln is synonymous with the Lancaster bomber and like Ely, the cathedral has special stained glass windows commemorating fallen RAF aircrew.

The aircraft demonstrate the importance that the RAF places upon maintaining these veterans in perfect flying condition and the desire to maintain a tangible link with the past. Above all they remember the national debt owed to those who paid the ultimate sacrifice.

AIRCRAFT OF
THE MEMORIAL FLIGHT

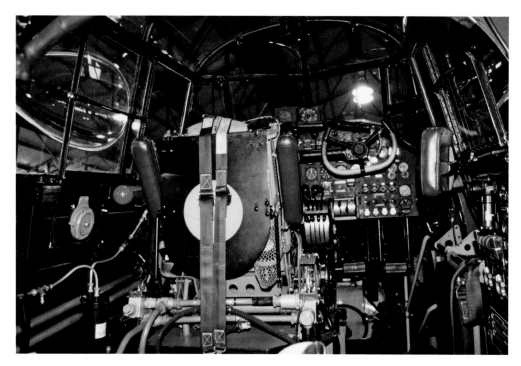

"From August until the end of September 1943 Lancasters were continually involved in bombing raids over German cities. Three raids against Berlin totalled almost 1000 aircraft while a similar number were involved in raids including Nuremberg, Mannheim and Hanover. The continuous effort brought inevitable losses, including 22 brought down over Berlin on the night of 3/4 September. How the crews survived under such pressure only they will know."

THE HURRICANES

"Hurricane D 1 hour, 30 minutes. Intercepted 100 E/A bombers at 15,000 feet. Was up-sun and above them. Dived the whole squadron into attack from above and behind. Squadron destroyed 12 E/A for loss of none. Self 2 Me 110s. No bullet holes in any aeroplane."

Squadron Leader Douglas Bader, Commanding 242 Squadron,
log book entry 30 August 1940.

The first and only Victoria Cross ever awarded to a Fighter Command pilot was won by Ft Lt James Nicolson, a Hurricane pilot of No 249 Squadron who, on August 16,1940, while attacking a German aircraft, was pounced on from above and behind by other German aircraft. Nicolson's aircraft caught fire, but he continued his attack until he had shot down his original target, then parachuted to safety.

"Coo! What a blitz! Patrol base.
All of a sudden we sight a cloud of
Huns and move unwillingly towards
them, but sight another cloud
complete with mosquitoes a bit
nearer; we move even more unwillingly towards them and attack.
Everyone takes a swing at the 50
Dornier 215s and the Messerschmitt
109s. Hell of a lot of zigging. Very
hectic. Day's bag nine 109s, three
215s."

Squadron Leader Michael Nicholson
Crossley, Hurricane I pilot, 32 Squadron,
Monday 12 August 1940. From *So Few:
The Immortal Record of the Royal Air Force*
by David Masters (1941)

"*Whenever a new fighter was flying Mitchell would get into his car and drive from his office in Eastleigh. As I was coming into land I would see his yellow Rolls Royce parked and know he was there. He once said 'Look, I'll give you a bit of advice Jeffrey. If anyone ever tells you anything about an aeroplane that is so bloody complicated you can't understand it, take it from me, it's all balls!'*"

Test pilot Jeffrey Quill remembers R J Mitchell.

"I had a quick bang at one of the enemy, then at another. Then I happened to turn up sun and joined two aircraft that were climbing, when I discovered that I was following two Messerschmitt 109s at only a few yards distance; in fact, I was formating on them. By the time I'd realised my mistake they had turned away from the sun and I opened fire on the leader. I came up behind him and gave him a burst and he dropped down into the Channel. When I gave the second one a burst he just exploded in mid-air."

Flight Lieutenant Harbourne Mackay Stephen, 74 Squadron 11 August 1940. *So Few: The Immortal Record of the Royal Air Force* by David Masters (1941)

"Against a gradually lightening sky, the fleeting
shadows of the fighters become sharper as they sweep over
their sector in stacked groups crowding in between the
water and the clouds. On this invasion day our pilots
lived intensely from dawn to dusk."

Jean Accart

43

'THE LAST!'

"War. A dangerous game played with no rule book, it rested on the individual - individual responsibility in leadership with faith and courage, so that the sense of belonging to a great Service in its hour of triumph lifted the spirit above the horror and bestiality of war."

Group Captain W.G.G. Duncan Smith

"*At first the speed amazed me. I was frightened out of my life and absolutely scared to do other than fly straight and level. This soon wore off, and before long Spitfires were being aerobated to the utmost. A Spitfire is the most beautiful and easy aircraft to fly and has no tricks or peculiarities normally attributable to high speed fighters.*"

Alan Deere's reactions the first time
he sat in a Spitfire in February, 1940

"The important thing with any photographic sortie was to take the pictures if one could and get them back to base. As Wing Commander Geoffrey Tuttle often used to say 'I want you to get home safely not because I like your faces, but because if you don't the whole sortie will be a waste of time!'"

Pilot Officer Gordon Green, PRU

DOUGLAS DC-3 DAKOTA

THE LANCASTER

"Our load was 18 five-hundreds and a cookie. Off we went and we got some flak over the Channel Islands. The WOp, Harry Hannah, was not at all keen on having a big hole in the floor of J-Johnny and when he went to the Elsan he clung to the fuselage like a rock climber. Approaching the target there was a lot of light flak then suddenly we were caught by searchlights. I'd got a smoked Perspex screen over my goggles so I wasn't dazzled even though the inside of J-Johnny looked like it had been whitewashed. Phil was on his run and the bombs went, more or less as I fired at the searchlights. He and the mid-upper, Sergeant Corr who was right above me, both said, 'Christ, what the hell was that?' and the searchlights went out. Now, I don't think I shot them out although everybody said I did. I think Ron Mathers, who was just behind us, had hit them with his bombs."

Mick Maguire, 9 Squadron Armaments Officer, W4964 J-Johnny, Lanveoc airfield, France, 8 May 1944.
W4964 'Still Going Strong!' of 9 Squadron flew 106 ops between April 1943 and October

62

PART TWO
THE SPEECH THAT LAUNCHED 'THE FEW'

At 3.52 pm on Tuesday August 20 1940, Winston Churchill rose to his feet in the House of Commons. His task was to deliver a Prime Ministerial assessment of the progress of the war and this he did at length and, as would be expected, in colourful sentences and phrases.

One especially vivid passage has remained in our consciousness ever since though it was not the climax of the speech.

Churchill declared, "The gratitude of every home in our Island, in our Empire, and indeed throughout the world, except in the abodes of the guilty, goes out to the British airmen who, undaunted by odds, unwearied in their constant challenge and mortal danger, are turning the tide of the World War by their prowess and by their devotion. Never in the field of human conflict was so much owed by so many to so few."

So the legend of The Few was born, the men of the RAF who were the spearhead of British defence at a time when invasion was a distinct possibility.

From the vantage point of the 21st century, we know that victory over Germany was achieved both in "The Battle of Britain" and in the war as a whole. We know too that Winston Leonard Spencer Churchill would be acclaimed as a great war leader and as one of the towering figures of the century.

That these things should come to pass were far from certain in August 1940.

Churchill had returned to Government after his "wilderness years" on the outbreak of war. On September 1 1939 the then Prime Minister, Neville Chamberlain offered him a place in the War Cabinet. At first the nature of that place was not clear. Two days later Churchill learned that he was in fact to be First Lord of the Admiralty, an office he had also held, amidst great controversy, in the Great War.

In April 1940 Britain and France went to the aid of Norway, suffering under German invasion. The campaign was not a success and a two day "inquest" took place in the House of Commons on May 7 and 8. This, "was by a clear head the most dramatic and the most far-reaching in its consequences of any parliamentary debate of the 20th century," wrote Roy Jenkins, a Churchill biographer, who would witness and participate in his own fair share of Parliamentary drama.

Churchill was clearly one of those with responsibility for what had gone wrong, but speakers in the debate were inclined to argue that his talents had been misdirected by Chamberlain.

On a motion to adjourn the house, the nominal Conservative majority of 213 was reduced to 81. Chamberlain had both won and been, in political terms, fatally wounded.

Two days later Churchill was Prime Minister, beating off a not entirely whole-hearted challenge for the post from Lord Halifax. On the same day the German blitzkrieg began.

Churchill's position was far from secure in the early days of his Premiership. He struggled to keep France in the war and Italy out of it. He presided over the retreat of the British Expeditionary Force to the Channel ports and the "miracle of Dunkirk". All this against a background where some expected his time as Prime Minister to be short and some of his war cabinet were uncertain that his approach was best. Halifax could certainly see the attractions of discussing terms with Germany.

By July things were a little easier and Churchill a little more in control. We now say that the Battle of Britain began on July 10, though a definition using that date was not established for five years. The significance later attributed to this arbitrary point in the calendar was not apparent at the time. There was fighting over the Channel and southern England before that in what most of the participants would have seen as a continuation of what had been going on since Dunkirk.

On July 8, for example, a Messerscmitt Bf 109 forced-landed on Bladbean Hill outside the Kent village of Elham, having fallen to the guns of a Spitfire flown by Sergeant Edward Mould of No 74 Squadron. RAF casualties that day included Squadron Leader Desmond Cooke, the CO of No 65 Squadron, shot down near Dover. The following day, three more RAF fighter pilots were killed in action.

With invasion as the goal, the Luftwaffe was given the task of eliminating RAF Fighter Command as a threat to the planned landings.

By August 20, the early period of the Battle, involving much fighting over convoys in the Channel, had passed. So too had the German's Adler Tag (Eagle Day) on which, it was intended, the final annihilation of Fighter Command would begin. This attack finally occurred on August 13 and its dismal failure can, in large part, be attributed to the remarkably poor German intelligence on airfields appropriate for their attention.

August 18 is sometimes called the RAF's "Hardest Day", with major attacks on the airfields at Kenley and Biggin Hill, but when Churchill made his speech the full weight of the airfield attacks, as well as the fighting over London, were still in the future. The Battle of Britain would end officially on October 31, though that was also something that went utterly unremarked at the time.

"Almost a year has passed since the war began," Churchill started, "and it is natural I think for us to pause on our journey at this milestone and survey the dark wide field."

Churchill contrasted the current experience with that of the first year of the earlier World War, noting the much smaller casualty rate. He claimed greater scientific competence for the allied side, "Since the Germans drove the Jews out and lowered their technical standards". He spoke of the advantages of Britain's geographical position and "command of the sea" and vaunted the friendship of the United States.

He continued to range over the events of the war and the impact of Government policies amongst them. The ability of the Ministry of Aircraft Production (established against much RAF opposition) to return damaged aircraft to the fighting was praised and the increase in aircraft production was said to be, "splendid, nay astounding".

Then, about two thirds of the way through, came the famous words.

It is important to note precisely what was said immediately after, "so few".

" All hearts go out to the fighter pilots, whose brilliant actions we see with our own eyes day after day; but we must never forget that all the time, night after night, month after month, our bomber squadrons travel far into Germany, find their targets in the darkness by the highest navigational skill, aim their attacks, often under the heaviest fire, often with serious loss, with deliberate careful discrimination, and inflict shattering blows upon the whole of the technical and war-making structure of the Nazi power. On no part of the Royal Air Force does the weight of the war fall more heavily than on the daylight bombers, who will play an invaluable part in the case of invasion and whose unflinching zeal it has been necessary in the meanwhile on numerous occasions to restrain."

This passage is perhaps what has led many to argue that in creating the concept of "The Few" of the RAF the Prime Minister was referring, not only to Fighter Command, but to Bomber Command and perhaps even Coastal Command, as well, whose aircraft were taking part in the bombing.

One at the time who did not accept that argument was Air Chief Marshal Dowding the head of Fighter Command. In the emotional letter that he sent to "My Dear Fighter Boys" as he left his command in November 1940, Dowding made it clear that he believed that Churchill had been referring to Fighter Command.

A view on the subject was expressed by Churchill himself. Writing in *The Second World War*, vol ll, 'Their Finest Hour', published in 1949, he declared, "At the summit (of endeavour in the Battle of Britain) the stamina and valour of our fighter pilots remained unconquerable and supreme. Thus Britain was saved, well might I say in the House of Commons, 'Never in the field of human conflict was so much owed by so many to so few.'"

Geoff Simpson
2010

WINSTON CHURCHILL'S SPEECH

DELIVERED IN THE HOUSE OF COMMONS 20 AUGUST 1940

Almost a year has passed since the war began, and it is natural for us, I think, to pause on our journey at this milestone and survey the dark, wide field. It is also useful to compare the first year of this second war against German aggression with its forerunner a quarter of a century ago. Although this war is in fact only a continuation of the last, very great differences in its character are apparent. In the last war millions of men fought by hurling enormous masses of steel at one another. "Men and shells" was the cry, and prodigious slaughter was the consequence. In this war nothing of this kind has yet appeared. It is a conflict of strategy, of organization, of technical apparatus, of science, mechanics and morale. The British casualties in the first 12 months of the Great War amounted to 365,000. In this war, I am thankful to say, British killed, wounded, prisoners and missing, including civilians, do not exceed 92,000, and of these a large proportion are alive as prisoners of war. Looking more widely around, one may say that throughout all Europe, for one man killed or wounded in the first year perhaps five were killed or wounded in 1914-15.

The slaughter is only a small fraction, but the consequences to the belligerents have been even more deadly. We have seen great countries with powerful armies dashed out of coherent existence in a few weeks. We have seen the French Republic and the renowned French Army beaten into complete and total submission with less than the casualties which they suffered in any one of half a dozen of the battles of 1914-18. The entire body - it might almost seem at times the soul - of France has succumbed to physical effects incomparably less terrible than those which were sustained with fortitude and undaunted will power 25 years ago. Although up to the present the loss of life has been mercifully diminished, the decisions reached in the course of the struggle are even more profound upon the fate of nations than anything that has ever happened since barbaric times. Moves are made upon the scientific and strategic boards, advantages are gained by mechanical means, as a result of which scores of millions of men become incapable of further resistance, or judge themselves incapable of further resistance, and a fearful game of chess proceeds from check to mate by which the unhappy players seem to be inexorably bound.

There is another more obvious difference from 1914. The whole of the warring nations are engaged, not only soldiers, but the entire population, men, women and children. The fronts are everywhere. The trenches are dug in the towns and streets. Every village is fortified. Every road is barred. The front line runs through the factories. The workmen are soldiers with different weapons but the same courage. These are great and distinctive changes from what many of us saw in the struggle of a quarter of a century ago. There seems to be every reason to believe that this new kind of war is well suited to the genius and the resources of the British nation and the British Empire; and that, once we get properly equipped and properly started, a war of this kind will be more favorable to us than the sombre mass slaughters of the Somme and Passchendaele. If it is a case of the whole nation fighting and suffering together, that ought to suit us, because we are the most united of all the nations, because we entered the war upon the national will and with our eyes open, and because we have been nurtured in freedom and individual responsibility and are the products, not of totalitarian uniformity, but of tolerance and variety. If all these qualities are turned, as they are being turned, to the arts of war, we may be able to show the enemy quite a lot of things that they have not thought of yet. Since the Germans drove the Jews out and lowered their technical standards, our science is definitely ahead of theirs. Our geographical position, the command of the sea, and the friendship of the United States enable us to draw resources from the whole world and to manufacture weapons of war of every kind, but especially of the superfine kinds, on a scale hitherto practiced only by Nazi Germany. Hitler is now sprawled over Europe. Our offensive springs are being slowly compressed, and we must resolutely and methodically prepare ourselves for the campaigns of 1941 and 1942. Two or three years are not a long time, even in our short, precarious lives. They are nothing in the history of the nation, and when we are doing the finest thing in the world, and have the honor to be the sole champion of the liberties of all Europe, we must not grudge these years or weary as we toil and struggle through them. It does not follow that our energies in future years will be exclusively confined to defending ourselves and our possessions. Many opportunities may lie open to amphibious power, and we must be ready to take advantage of them. One of the ways to bring this war to a speedy end is to convince the enemy, not by words, but by deeds, that we have both the will and the means, not only to go on indefinitely, but to strike heavy and unexpected blows. The road to victory may not be so long as we expect. But we have no right to count upon this. Be it long or short, rough or smooth, we mean to reach our journey's end.

It is our intention to maintain and enforce a strict blockade, not only of Germany, but of Italy, France, and all the other countries that have fallen

into the German power. I read in the papers that Herr Hitler has also proclaimed a strict blockade of the British Islands. No one can complain of that. I remember the Kaiser doing it in the last war. What indeed would be a matter of general complaint would be if we were to prolong the agony of all Europe by allowing food to come in to nourish the Nazis and aid their war effort, or to allow food to go in to the subjugated peoples, which certainly would be pillaged off them by their Nazi conquerors.

There have been many proposals, founded on the highest motives, that food should be allowed to pass the blockade for the relief of these populations. I regret that we must refuse these requests. The Nazis declare that they have created a new unified economy in Europe. They have repeatedly stated that they possess ample reserves of food and that they can feed their captive peoples. In a German broadcast of 27th June it was said that while Mr. Hoover's plan for

relieving France, Belgium and Holland deserved commendation, the German forces had already taken the necessary steps. We know that in Norway when the German troops went in, there were food supplies to last for a year. We know that Poland, though not a rich country, usually produces sufficient food for her people. Moreover, the other countries which Herr Hitler has invaded all held considerable stocks when the Germans entered and are themselves, in many cases, very substantial food producers. If all this food is not available now, it can only be because it has been removed to feed the people of Germany and to give them increased rations - for a change - during the last few months. At this season of the year and for some months to come, there is the least chance of scarcity as the harvest has just been gathered in. The only agencies which can create famine in any part of Europe, now and during the coming winter, will be German exactions or German failure to distribute the supplies which they command.

There is another aspect. Many of the most valuable foods are essential to the manufacture of vital war material. Fats are used to make explosives. Potatoes make the alcohol for motor spirit. The plastic materials now so largely used in the construction of aircraft are made of milk. If the Germans use these commodities to help them to bomb our women and children,

66

rather than to feed the populations who produce them, we may be sure that imported foods would go the same way, directly or indirectly, or be employed to relieve the enemy of the responsibilities he has so wantonly assumed. Let Hitler bear his responsibilities to the full, and let the peoples of Europe who groan beneath his yoke aid in every way the coming of the day when that yoke will be broken. Meanwhile, we can and we will arrange in advance for the speedy entry of food into any part of the enslaved area, when this part has been wholly cleared of German forces, and has genuinely regained its freedom. We shall do our best to encourage the building up of reserves of food all over the world, so that there will always be held up before the eyes of the peoples of Europe, including - I say deliberately - the German and Austrian peoples, the certainty that the shattering of the Nazi power will bring to them all immediate food, freedom and peace.

Rather more than a quarter of a year has passed since the new Government came into power in this country. What a cataract of disaster has poured out upon us since then! The trustful Dutch overwhelmed; their beloved and respected Sovereign driven into exile; the peaceful city of Rotterdam the scene of a massacre as hideous and brutal as anything in the Thirty Years' War; Belgium invaded and beaten down; our own fine Expeditionary Force, which King Leopold called to his rescue, cut off and almost captured, escaping as it seemed only by a miracle and with the loss of all its equipment; our Ally, France, out; Italy in against us; all France in the power of the enemy, all its arsenals and vast masses of military material converted or convertible to the enemy's use; a puppet Government set up at Vichy which may at any moment be forced to become our foe; the whole western seaboard of Europe from the North Cape to the Spanish frontier in German hands; all the ports, all the airfields on this immense front employed against us as potential springboards of invasion. Moreover, the German air power, numerically so far outstripping ours, has been brought so close to our Island that what we used to dread greatly has come to pass and the hostile bombers not only reach our shores in a few minutes and from many directions, but can be escorted by their fighting aircraft. Why, Sir, if we had been confronted at the beginning of May with such a prospect, it would have seemed incredible that at the end of a period of horror and disaster, or at this point in a period of horror and disaster, we should stand erect, sure of ourselves, masters of our fate and with the conviction of final victory burning unquenchable in our hearts. Few would have believed we could survive; none would have believed that we should today not only feel stronger but should actually be stronger than we have ever been before.

Let us see what has happened on the other side of the scales. The British nation and the British Empire, finding themselves alone, stood undismayed against disaster. No one flinched or wavered; nay, some who formerly thought of peace,

now think only of war. Our people are united and resolved, as they have never been before. Death and ruin have become small things compared with the shame of defeat or failure in duty. We cannot tell what lies ahead. It may be that even greater ordeals lie before us. We shall face whatever is coming to us. We are sure of ourselves and of our cause, and that is the supreme fact which has emerged in these months of trial.

Meanwhile, we have not only fortified our hearts but our Island. We have rearmed and rebuilt our armies in a degree which would have been deemed impossible a few months ago. We have ferried across the Atlantic, in the month of July, thanks to our friends over there, an immense mass of munitions of all kinds: cannon, rifles, machine guns, cartridges and shell, all safely landed without the loss of a gun or a round. The output of our own factories, working as they have never worked before, has poured forth to the troops. The whole British Army is at home. More than 2,000,000 determined men have rifles and bayonets in their hands tonight, and three-quarters of them are in regular military formations. We have never had armies like this in our Island in time of war. The whole Island bristles against invaders, from the sea or from the air. As I explained to the House in the middle of June, the stronger our Army at home, the larger must the invading expedition be, and the larger the invading expedition, the less difficult will be the task of the Navy in detecting its assembly and in intercepting and destroying it in passage; and the greater also would be the difficulty of feeding and supplying the invaders if ever they landed, in the teeth of continuous naval and air attack on their communications. All this is classical and venerable doctrine. As in Nelson's day, the maxim holds, "Our first line of defense is the enemy's ports." Now air reconnaissance and photography have brought to an old principle a new and potent aid.

Our Navy is far stronger than it was at the beginning of the war. The great flow of new construction set on foot at the outbreak is now beginning to come in. We hope our friends across the ocean will send us a timely reinforcement to bridge the gap between the peace flotillas of 1939 and the war flotillas of 1941. There is no difficulty in sending such aid. The seas and oceans are open. The U-boats are contained. The magnetic mine is, up to the present time, effectively mastered. The merchant tonnage under the British flag, after a year of unlimited U-boat war, after eight months of intensive mining attack, is larger than when we began. We have, in addition, under our control at least 4,000,000 tons of shipping from the captive countries which has taken refuge here or in the harbors of the Empire. Our stocks of food of all kinds are far more abundant than in the days of peace, and a large and growing programme of food production is on foot.

Why do I say all this? Not, assuredly, to boast; not, assuredly, to give the slightest countenance to complacency. The dangers we face are still enormous, but so are our advantages and resources. I recount them because the people have a right to know that there are solid grounds for the confidence which we feel, and that we have good reason to believe ourselves capable, as I said in a very dark hour two months ago, of continuing the war "if necessary alone, if necessary for years." I say it also because the fact that the British Empire stands invincible, and that Nazidom is still being resisted, will kindle again the spark of hope in the breasts of hundreds of millions of down-trodden or despairing men and women throughout Europe, and far beyond its bounds, and that from these sparks there will presently come cleansing and devouring flame. The great air battle which has been in progress over this Island for the last few weeks has recently attained a high intensity. It is too soon to attempt to assign limits either to its scale or to its duration. We must certainly expect that greater efforts will be made by the enemy than any he has so far put forth. Hostile air fields are still being developed in France and the Low Countries, and the movement of squadrons and material for attacking us is still proceeding. It is quite plain that Herr Hitler could not admit defeat in his air attack on Great Britain without sustaining most serious injury. If after all his boastings and bloodcurdling threats and lurid accounts trumpeted round the world of the damage he has inflicted, of the vast numbers of our Air Force he has shot down, so he says, with so little loss to himself; if after tales of the panic-stricken British crushed in their holes cursing the plutocratic Parliament which has led them to such a plight - if after all this his whole air onslaught were forced after a while tamely to peter out, the Fuhrer's reputation for veracity of statement might be seriously impugned. We may be sure, therefore, that he will continue as long as he has the strength to do so, and as long as any preoccupations he may have in respect of the Russian Air Force allow him to do so. On the other hand, the conditions and course of the fighting have so far been favorable to us. I told the House two months ago that, whereas in France our fighter aircraft were wont to inflict a loss of two or three to one upon the Germans, and in the fighting at Dunkirk, which was a kind of no-man's-land, a loss of about three or four to one, we expected that in an attack on this Island we should achieve a larger ratio. This has certainly come true. It must also be remembered that all the enemy machines and pilots which are shot down over our Island, or over the seas which surround it, are either destroyed or captured; whereas a considerable proportion of our machines, and also of our pilots, are saved, and soon again in many cases come into action.

A vast and admirable system of salvage, directed by the Ministry of Aircraft Production, ensures the speediest return to the fighting line of damaged machines, and the most provident and speedy use of all the spare parts and material. At the same time the splendid - nay, astounding - increase in the output and repair of British aircraft and engines which Lord Beaverbrook has achieved by a genius of organization and drive, which looks like magic, has given us overflowing reserves of every type of aircraft, and an ever-mounting stream of production both in quantity and quality. The enemy is, of course, far more numerous than we are. But our new production already, as I am advised, largely exceeds his, and the American production is only just beginning to flow in. It is a fact, as I see from my daily returns, that our bomber and fighter strength now, after all this fighting, are larger than they have ever been. We believe that we shall be able to continue the air struggle indefinitely and as long as the enemy pleases, and the longer it continues the more rapid will be our approach, first towards that parity, and then into that superiority, in the air upon which in a large measure the decision of the war depends.

The gratitude of every home in our Island, in our Empire, and indeed throughout the world, except in the abodes of the guilty, goes out to the British airmen who, undaunted by odds, unwearied in their constant challenge and mortal danger, are turning the tide of the World War by their prowess and by their devotion. Never in the field of human conflict was so much owed by so many to so few. All hearts go out to the fighter pilots, whose brilliant actions we see with our own eyes day after day; but we must never forget that all the time, night after night, month after month, our bomber squadrons travel far into Germany, find their targets in the darkness by the highest navigational skill, aim their attacks, often under the heaviest fire, often with serious loss, with deliberate careful discrimination, and inflict shattering blows upon the whole of the technical and war-making structure of the Nazi power. On no part of the Royal Air Force does the weight of the war fall more heavily than on the daylight bombers, who will play an invaluable part in the case of invasion and whose unflinching zeal it has been necessary in the meanwhile on numerous occasions to restrain.

We are able to verify the results of bombing military targets in Germany, not only by reports which reach us through many sources, but also, of course, by photography. I have no hesitation in saying that this process of bombing the military industries and communications of Germany and the air bases and storage depots from which we are attacked, which process will continue upon an ever-increasing scale until the end of the war, and may in another year attain dimensions hitherto undreamed of, affords one at least of the most certain, if not the shortest, of all the roads to victory. Even if the Nazi legions stood triumphant on the Black Sea, or indeed upon the Caspian, even if Hitler was at the gates of India, it would profit him nothing if at the same time the entire economic and scientific apparatus of German war power lay shattered and pulverized at home.

The fact that the invasion of this Island upon a large scale has become a far more difficult operation with every week that has passed since we saved our Army at Dunkirk, and our very great preponderance of sea power enable us to turn our eyes and to turn our strength increasingly towards the Mediterranean and against that other enemy who, without the slightest provocation, coldly and deliberately, for greed and gain, stabbed France in the back in the moment of her agony, and is now marching against us in Africa. The defection of France has, of course, been deeply damaging to our position in what is called, somewhat oddly, the Middle East. In the defense of Somaliland, for instance, we had counted upon strong French forces attacking the Italians from Jibuti. We had counted also upon the use of the French naval and air bases in the Mediterranean, and particularly upon the North African shore. We had counted upon the French Fleet. Even though metropolitan France was temporarily overrun, there was no reason why the French Navy, substantial parts of the French Army, the French Air Force and the French Empire over-seas should not have continued the struggle at our side.

Shielded by overwhelming sea power, possessed of invaluable strategic bases and of ample funds, France might have remained one of the great combatants in the struggle. By so doing, France would have preserved the continuity of her life, and the French Empire might have advanced with the British Empire to the rescue of the independence and integrity of the French Motherland. In our own case, if we had been put in the terrible position of France, a contingency now happily impossible, although, of course, it would have been the duty of all war leaders to fight on here to the end, it would also have been their duty, as I indicated in my speech of 4th June, to provide as far as possible for the Naval security of Canada and our Dominions and to make sure they had the means to carry on the struggle from beyond the oceans. Most of the other countries that have been overrun by Germany for the time being have persevered valiantly and faithfully. The Czechs, the Poles, the Norwegians, the Dutch, the Belgians are still in the field, sword in hand, recognized by Great Britain and the United States as the sole representative authorities and lawful Governments of their respective States.

That France alone should lie prostrate at this moment is the crime, not of a great and noble nation, but of what are called "the men of Vichy." We have profound sympathy with the French people. Our old comradeship with France is not dead. In General de Gaulle and his gallant band, that comradeship takes an effective form. These free Frenchmen have been condemned to death by Vichy, but the day will come, as surely as the sun will rise tomorrow, when their names will be held in honour, and their names will be graven in stone in the streets and villages of a France restored in a liberated Europe to its full freedom and its ancient fame. But this conviction which I feel of the future cannot affect the immediate problems which confront us in the Mediterranean

Sir Winston Churchill, 1946, Oil on canvas by Douglas Granville Chandor

and in Africa. It had been decided some time before the beginning of the war not to defend the Protectorate of Somaliland. That policy was changed in the early months of the war. When the French gave in, and when our small forces there, a few battalions, a few guns, were attacked by all the Italian troops, nearly two divisions, which had formerly faced the French at Jibuti, it was right to withdraw our detachments, virtually intact, for action elsewhere. Far larger operations no doubt impend in the Middle East theatre, and I shall certainly not attempt to discuss or prophesy about their probable course. We have large armies and many means of reinforcing them. We have the complete sea command of the eastern Mediterranean. We intend to do our best to give a *good account of ourselves, and to discharge faithfully and resolutely all our obligations and duties in that quarter of the world. More than that I do not think the House would wish me to say at the present time.*

A good many people have written to me to ask me to make on this occasion a fuller statement of our war aims, and of the kind of peace we wish to make after the war, than is contained in the very considerable declaration which was made early in the autumn. Since then we have made common cause with Norway, Holland and Belgium. We have recognized the Czech Government of Dr. Benes, and we have told General de Gaulle that our success will carry with it the restoration of France. I do not think it would be wise at this moment, while the battle rages and the war is still perhaps only in its earlier stage, to embark upon elaborate speculations about the future shape which should be given to Europe or the new securities which must be arranged to spare mankind the miseries of a third World War. The ground is not new, it has been frequently traversed and explored, and many ideas are held about it in common by all good men, and all free men. But before we can undertake the task of rebuilding we have not only to be convinced ourselves, but we have to convince all other countries that the Nazi tyranny is going to be finally broken. The right to guide the course of world history is the noblest prize of victory. We are still toiling up the hill; we have not yet reached the crest-line of it; we cannot survey the landscape or even imagine what its condition will be when that longed-for morning comes. The task which lies before us immediately is at once more practical, more simple and more stern. I hope - indeed, I pray - that we shall not be found unworthy of our victory if after toil and tribulation it is granted to us. For the rest, we have to gain the victory. That is our task. There is, however, one direction in which we can see a little more clearly ahead. We have to think not only for ourselves but for the lasting security of the cause and principles for which we are fighting and of the long future of the British Commonwealth of Nations. Some months ago we came to the conclusion that the interests of the United States and of the British Empire both required that the United States should have facilities for the naval and air defence of the Western Hemisphere against the attack of a Nazi power which might have acquired temporary but lengthy control of a large part of Western Europe and its formidable resources. We had therefore decided spontaneously, and without being asked or offered any inducement, to inform the Government of the United States that we would be glad to place such defense facilities at their disposal by leasing suitable sites in our Transatlantic possessions for their greater security against the unmeasured dangers of the future. The principle of association of interests for common purposes between Great Britain and the United States had developed even before the war. Various agreements had been reached about certain small islands in the Pacific Ocean which had become important as air fueling points. In all this line of thought we found ourselves in very close harmony with the Government of Canada.

Presently we learned that anxiety was also felt in the United States about the air and naval defense of their Atlantic seaboard, and President Roosevelt has recently made it clear that he would like to discuss with us, and with the Dominion of Canada and with Newfoundland, the development of American naval and air facilities in Newfoundland and in the West Indies. There is, of course, no question of any transference of sovereignty - that has never been suggested - or of any action being taken without the consent or against the wishes of the various Colonies concerned; but for our part, His Majesty's Government are entirely willing to accord defense facilities to the United States on a 99 years' leasehold basis, and we feel sure that our interests no less than theirs, and the interests of the Colonies themselves and of Canada and Newfoundland, will be served thereby. These are important steps. Undoubtedly this process means that these two great organizations of the English-speaking democracies, the British Empire and the United States, will have to be some-what mixed up together in some of their affairs for mutual and general advantage. For my own part, looking out upon the future, I do not view the process with any misgivings. I could not stop it if I wished; no one can stop it. Like the Mississippi, it just keeps rolling along. Let it roll. Let it roll on full flood, inexorable, irresistible, benignant, to broader lands and better days.

PART THREE
REFLECTIONS AND RECOLLECTIONS

The following pages recall events from the Battle of Britain and the years following in which the aerial war over Europe was fought against the Axis forces. These stories, together with contemporary images and Martin Bowman's photographs of the Battle of Britain Memorial Flight, are stirring reminders of the men and machines that helped pave the way to ultimate victory.

DUXFORD AND DOUGLAS BADER

At Duxford on 1 July 1940, 19 Squadron's strength, officially, was only eight aircraft (with five unserviceable). On the same date 264 Squadron had 11 Defiants available. It was the same story everywhere. To meet the massive threat posed by the Luftwaffe in the Battle of Britain, ACM Sir Hugh 'Stuffy' Dowding's RAF Fighter Command numbered just 57 squadrons in three Groups. 11 Group in southern England commanded by AVM Keith Park had 29 squadrons. 12 Group (of which Duxford and Coltishall were two of its five airfields) commanded by AVM Sir Trafford Leigh-Mallory, had 11 fighter squadrons equipped with only 113 serviceable Spitfires, Defiants, Hurricanes and Blenheim Ifs. 13 Group, which covered the north-east, had 17 squadrons. The odds were stacked in Germany's favour, a point forcibly made on 20 August by British Prime Minster Winston Churchill.

'The gratitude of every home in our island, in our Empire and, indeed, throughout the world, except in the abodes of the guilty, goes out to the British airmen, who, undaunted by odds, unweary in their constant challenge and mortal danger, are turning the tide of the world war by their prowess and their devotion. Never in the field of human conflict was so much owed by so many to so few.'

On 30 August the *Luftwaffe* began a 48-hour assault on Fighter Command's Sector stations. 11 Group was threatened with being overrun by sheer weight of numbers and 12 Group had to act as an airborne reserve for them. Early that morning 242 Squadron, commanded by Squadron Leader Douglas Bader at Coltishall was scrambled but was recalled while en route to Duxford. Ordered off again, the Hurricanes were in position by 10:00 hours. At Duxford the Station Commander, Group Captain A. B. 'Woody' Woodhall the fighter controller ordered '242 Squadron scramble! Angels 15. North Weald.' Bader ignored the request to 'Vector one-nine-zero. Buster', flying 30° further west to get up-sun. When he spotted 50 Dorniers escorted by Bf 110s bearing down on North Weald, Bader led 242 down into the German formation and the Hurricanes routed them. Twelve enemy bombers were shot down and North Weald escaped destruction but the Vauxhall Motor Works at Luton was badly hit and 53 civilians killed and 60 injured. Altogether, the day's fighting cost the RAF 26 fighters shot down and the Luftwaffe 36.

Back at Coltishall Bader was congratulated by the AOC 12 Group. Bader argued that with more fighters they could have shot down three times the number. In theory, a large fighter formation could he brought to bear on the enemy formations thereby increasing the chances of 'knocking down' more aircraft than smaller numbers were capable of doing. Leigh-Mallory had long held the belief that a 'Wing' could achieve greater killing potential than the squadron formations favoured by Dowding and by Park, who had much less time to form up squadrons into Wings.

On 31 August 242 Squadron were scrambled three times to patrol North London once more, but they found nothing. Fighter Command lost 39 fighters and Debden, Biggin Hill, Manston, West Malling, Hawkinge, Hornchurch, and Lympne got a pasting from Luftwaffe bombers. Duxford was only saved by Squadron Leader J. M. 'Tommy' Thompson's 111 Squadron from Debden. South of the Thames only two RAF Sector stations were still operational. Leigh-Mallory landed at Coltishall and talked 'Wings' to Bader between patrols. The commander told Bader that, starting on the morrow, 242 and 310 (Czech) Squadrons' Hurricanes would use Duxford daily. Together with 19 Squadron operating out of the satellite at Fowlmere, they would form the 'Big Wing'.

At first there was no 'trade' for Bader to pursue. He practiced with the 'Duxford Wing' for four days and reduced take-off times to just three minutes, the same as a squadron, but they

were not called into action. On 5 September 19 Squadron lost three Spitfires and the CO, Squadron Leader P. C. Pinkham AFC was killed. Squadron Leader Brian J. 'Sandy' Lane DFC took over command. On 6 September six of 11 Group's seven sector stations and five of its advanced airfields were very badly damaged. With the sector stations expecting annihilation and a signal being sent that an invasion was imminent, on 7 September the Luftwaffe inexplicably switched its daylight attacks, sending 300 bombers to bomb London. Woodhall asked Bader to 'Orbit North Weald. Angels 10'. He went instead to 'Angels 15', but was still below the enemy formation when it was sighted heading for the capital. Although 19 and 310 Squadrons never did catch up with 242 Squadron, 'Bader's Bus Company' claimed 11 enemy aircraft for the loss of two Hurricanes, though one pilot was safe.

Next morning 242 Squadron flew to Duxford, where Bader and his pilots spent a frustrating day waiting in vain to be summoned by 11

Group. The same thing happened on the 9th, until at 17:00 hours it was announced that radar had detected a build-up of German aircraft over the Pas de Calais. Only when the bombers headed in were the Hurricanes permitted to scramble. Woodhall asked Bader, 'Will you patrol between North Weald and Hornchurch, Angels 20?' Bader disregarded this and climbed southwest to 22,000ft. When he sighted the bombers he ordered 19 Squadron's Spitfires to climb higher and provide cover as the Hurricanes attacked in line astern through the middle of the enemy bomber formation. The 'Duxford Wing' routed the bombers and claimed 11 of the 28 officially destroyed this day. Three Hurricanes of 310 Squadron failed to return and two Hurricanes of 242 Squadron were shot down.

On 13 September Bader, who was awarded the DSO, was given 302 Polish with Hurricanes and 611 Squadron with Spitfires to bring the Wing up to 60 fighters, joining 242, 310 and 19 Squadrons at Duxford and Fowlmere. Twice the 'Duxford Wing' patrolled North London; to no avail. On Sunday 15 September the first wave of Luftwaffe aircraft plotted heading for London were engaged by 11 Group. When the next wave came in the five-squadron wing was summoned to action by 11 Group, now badly in need of reinforcements. Woodhall asked Bader to patrol Canterbury-Gravesend. He did, but though Sandy Lane's and 611 Squadron's Spitfires assailed the bombers, Bader's and the two other Hurricane squadrons were jumped by Bf 109s.

The Wing landed, refuelled, and was at readiness again by 11:45 hours. Two hours later the Wing was scrambled again. Flight Lieutenant George S. F. Powell-Sheddon was shot down by a Do 17 but was safe. Bader still complained of being scrambled too late. Arguments that 'Big Wings' were unwieldy seemed justified, especially when 11 Group's own

three-squadron 'Wing' of 32 fighters, led by Bob Stanford-Tuck from Debden, had only eight fighters remaining by the time they intercepted the bombers. The 'Duxford Wing' claimed 52 enemy aircraft shot down in the two engagements and eight probably destroyed. Overall, Fighter Command claimed to have shot down 185 aircraft, but the true figure was 56 shot down for the loss of 26 fighters.

On 18 September the Duxford Wing claimed 30 enemy aircraft destroyed, six probables and two damaged. 242 Squadron claimed 11 of these for no loss and 19 Squadron lost two Spitfires, though their pilots were safe. The last 'Big Wing' 'thrash' came on 27 September, when the Luftwaffe lost 55 aircraft, the RAF losing 28 fighters. Both 242 and 302 Squadrons lost one Hurricane each, 19 Squadron lost two Spitfires and 310 Squadron, one Hurricane. Total claims by the 'Duxford Wing' for 27 September were 12 destroyed. This took Bader's 'Big Wing' claims to 152 aircraft shot down for the loss of 30 pilots.

When the RAF turned to the offensive, 'the architects of victory', ACM Sir Hugh Dowding and ACM Sir Keith Park handed over to ACM Sir W. Sholto Douglas and ACM Sir Trafford Leigh-Mallory respectively. In March 1941 Sholto Douglas established the post of wing commander flying at all main airfields and Bader was given the Tangmere Wing. Bader was shot down and taken PoW on 9 August 1941. He had scored 20 and 4 shared victories.

'A Spitfire's just like a soft-mouthed, high-spirited thoroughbred.'

Squadron Leader Archibald Ashmore 'Archie' McKellar DSO DFC*
602 Squadron Spitfire I pilot,
October 1939

"Dowding made two vital contributions to the defeat of the Luftwaffe in the summer of 1940. Firstly during his pre-war command he laid down radar coverage of the south of England so that we had early warning of the German's intentions. Secondly, he had persuaded the War Cabinet against sending more RAF fighters to a defeated France in 1940."

Group Captain Sir Douglas Bader

A PILOT'S SCRAPBOOK

"Ten miles east of Duxford I was hit in the left leg by an explosive bullet from one of the Dorniers. Looking down I could see my foot hanging loose on the pedal. I still went in to open fire on a Dornier but immediately my cannon jammed. Instinctively I ducked as the top of my Spitfire grazed the underside of the enemy bomber. My cockpit hood was ripped away and the Spitfire spiralled down out of control, petrol spilling all over me. I bailed out at 22,000 feet and got caught on the back of the cockpit as I went. I finally freed myself and was going to free fall for a bit or I would have bled to death before I could land. But my foot was thrashing around by my thigh and the pain was too much to bear so I pulled the ripcord and swung there in a figure of eight."

Caricature of his fellow officers drawn by Coward.

"It was amazing how bright it was so high up. With every heartbeat I could see a gush of blood from my severed foot and at that height and in that cold thin air, the blood spread out almost pink in curious spirals. I used the radio wire from my helmet to put a tourniquet around my thigh. After that I felt no pain apart from the petrol that had drenched me and was stinging my armpits and crotch. I drifted across Duxford towards Fowlmere and then the wind took me back again and I landed in a stubble field near the Red Lion at Whittlesford. Eventually I was taken by ambulance to Addenbrooke's Hospital in Cambridge where my left leg was later amputated below the knee."

25-year old Flying Officer
James Baird Coward
19 Squadron, 31 August 1940.

Photograph inserted in Coward's Log Book.

On 29 December 1939 James had married Cynthia Bayon from Little Shelford, 4 miles from RAF Duxford.

"*Waiting for the phone call to 'scramble' into action was purgatory. With one eye constantly flickering to the telephone, you were like a cat on hot bricks, nervous, frightened. That's what I'm trying to say, scared stiff! The sound of the telephone ringing had everyone on tenterhooks.*"

Pilot Officer 'Boy' Geoffrey Wellum, 92 Squadron

"It was only by June or July that we began to learn the technique of air fighting and Wing Commander Malan was the greatest of leaders."

Flight Lieutenant Harbourne
Mackay Stephen, 74 Squadron

"I was attacking a Dornier. I had fired several bursts at the target when a bullet from the rear gunner pierced the bullet proof portion of the windscreen in line with my eyes. At the same time I was engulfed in smoke. Thinking I was on fire I started to leave the aircraft when I realised that there were no flames and that the smoke came from burning Glycol escaping from a damaged cooling system. I switched petrol and ignition off and found a large field in which I landed without damage. I was met by an Army officer and two soldiers in a Jeep. Leaving one to guard the aircraft, we went to North Weald where I spent the night. The next day I took a fitter and spares to the damaged Spitfire which was then repaired and I took off and flew back to Duxford, having been listed as missing for 24 hours because North Weald was well and truly bombed and all the phones were knocked out. The offending bullet was found in the bottom of the cockpit!"

Flight Sergeant George C.
'Grumpy' Unwin DFM,
19 Squadron
11 September 1940

D Day Duty

Built at Castle Bromwich in early 1944, Spitfire Vb MK356 was delivered to Digby and to 443"Hornet" Squadron, Royal Canadian Air Force (RCAF). Coded 21-V, these are the only markings ever worn operationally by this aircraft. Early that March Flying Officer (later General) Gordon E. Ockenden, an 'old' 20 year old from Vermillion, Alberta was a pilot in B Flight. On 11 March "Hornet" Squadron moved to Holmsley South, Hampshire to form 144 Canadian Wing (commanded by Wing Commander "Johnnie" Johnson), 2nd TAF, to prepare for the invasion of France. MK356 was allocated to 'B' Flight and on 18 March Ockenden flew the Mark for the first time.

After Armament Practice Camp at Hutton Cranswick, the squadron moved to Westhampnett on 8 April, flying its first operation on the 13th when they provided top cover escort for Bostons and Mitchells bombing Dieppe. On 14 April Gord Ockenden flew MK356 on its first 'op' (he flew it on 19 altogether), a 1 hour 50-minute *Rodeo*, Compeigne-Paris Rouen encountering light flak. On 22 April "Hornet" Squadron moved to Funtington in Sussex and by 15 May was at Ford near the Sussex coast ready for invasion duty.

One of the Spitfire Vs on 402 'Winnipeg Bear' Squadron RCAF, which first operated mainly in a fighter bomber role at this time, was AB910,

"*They were leaving white trails in the air. I thought I would just get up behind them to shoot them out of the sky, but I couldn't. They kept diving at me, just putting their noses down and sweeping up to their old level again like a switchback; but they did not fire or come within 400 yards of me. Once I got into their slipstream, and my perspex iced up instantly and I could not see anything at all. My screen became quite opaque and I had to open the hood to see where the two Huns had got to. I felt like a kite balloon being dived upon as my aircraft stood up at a ridiculous angle. In opening the hood I lost 1,000 feet, so I had to break off and come down without firing a shot, They were still patrolling when I went home.*"

George Harman Bennions, Spitfire pilot 41 Squadron.

which was taken on charge 1 February 1944. Flying Officer George B Lawson, a Canadian, recalls.

'We still had the Mark V Spitfires on charge at that time [the squadron changed to the Spitfire Mark IX in July and AB910 was taken on charge by 530TU at Hibaldstow on 20 July 1944]. We had clipped wing Mark Vs and as we were training for D Day, we were actually taking off and landing in the dark, which was a bit unusual for Spits. We were doing quite a bit of night flying so that we could handle the take-offs in the dark, be over the beachhead at dawn, stay there until dusk and land afterward. While training we still flew our regular missions. On 21 May my usual aircraft AE-H (EN767) was hit by flak during a sweep from the Douai coast at deck level. We were shooting up trains and gun posts, according to my logbook. My H was washed out; even the aerial mast was shot off. I received a new AE-H (AB910). This was the aircraft I flew on 6 June 1944 [on Beachhead cover (Eastern Area) 0945-1215 hours. Much

later that momentous day, 2200-2359 hours, Pilot Officer H. C. Nicholson flew Beachhead cover in AB910] It became one the one I flew regularly It was painted up with black and white stripes and it had clipped wings. Most of 402 Squadron aircraft had a red maple leaf on a white circle below the cockpit. I was over on D Day in the morning. I don't recall any combats between ourselves and other fighters but we saw lots of action on the ground and from battleships firing at us!"

On D Day+1, 7 June AB910 was flown on another Beachhead cover patrol by George Lawson, 0430-0710 hours and at 0940-1045 hours as a spare for another Beachhead cover by Pilot Officer K. E. Heggie. That same day George Ockenden flew two patrols, Bayeux to Caen. On the second patrol in MK356, four Bf 109Gs were attacked on the 'deck'. Gord chased one of the Messerschmitts and obtained strikes. Flight Lieutenant Hugh Russell finished it off. The 109 exploded and each pilot was credited with a half share. Gord Ockenden flew 130 ops and his

wartime score reached four confirmed victories, one shared destroyed, and one damaged. Russell was KIA on 16 June.

MK356 probably suffered two belly landings before the one that ended its flying career and was damaged by enemy action on three occasions. On 14 June it lost a wheel while taking off from Ford with Flying Officer "Gud" Monroe at the controls. Monroe continued the operation over France and on return made a belly landing. As the squadron moved to B-3 St. Croix-sur-Mer in France the next day MK356 was stored. Following the war, the aircraft was used for gate-guardian duties and also appeared as a static airframe in the film *The Battle of Britain* before going to St Athan. The aircraft's first flight for 53 years took place on 7 November 1997. A week later it was flown to its new home at Coningsby where it retains the same operational markings it wore in WWII.

LORD VC

Tuesday 19 September 1944 was a clear day in Holland and the besieged Red Berets of the British 1st Airborne Division at Arnhem looked forward to their resupply scheduled for 10.00am. At Down Ampney, thick mist delayed the take off of the C-47s of 271 Squadron until late in the day. At 1300 hours 17 Dakotas took off to resupply Drop Zone V on the northwestern outskirts of Arnhem but unknown to the crews, this DZ was already in German hands.

One of the Dakotas was KG374 flown by Flight Lieutenant David Lord DFC. Shortly before 1500 hours Lord began his descent into the swirling haze. At 1.500ft the Dakota broke out of cloud and was immediately hit in the starboard engine by flak and it burst into flames. The brave pilot would have been justified in leaving the main stream of supply aircraft and continuing at the same height or even abandoning his aircraft but on learning that his crew were uninjured and that the dropping zone would be reached in three minutes, Lord said he would complete his mission, as

"His task completed, Flight Lieutenant Lord ordered his crew to abandon the Dakota, making no attempt himself to leave the aircraft, which was down to 500 feet. A few seconds later, the starboard wing collapsed and the aircraft fell in flames. There was only one survivor, who was flung out while assisting other members of the crew to put on their parachutes."

"By continuing his mission in a damaged and burning aircraft, descending to drop the supplies accurately, returning to the dropping zone a second time and, finally, remaining at the controls to give his crew a chance of escape, Flight Lieutenant Lord displayed supreme valour and self-sacrifice."

From the full citation for Lord's VC
published in the *London Gazette* 9 November 1945

the paras were in dire need of supplies. By now the starboard engine was burning furiously. Lord went down to 900ft where he was singled out for the concentrated fire of all the AA guns. On reaching the dropping zone he kept the aircraft on a straight and level course while supplies were dropped. At the end of the run, he was told that two containers remained. Although he must have known that the collapse of the starboard wing would not be long delayed. Lord circled, rejoined the stream of aircraft and made a second run to drop the remaining supplies. These manoeuvres took eight minutes in all, the Dakota being continuously under heavy AA fire. His task completed, Lord ordered his crew to abandon the aircraft, making no attempt himself to leave the Dakota, which was down to 500ft. A few seconds later the aircraft fell in flames. There was only one survivor. Flying Officer Harry King, navigator was flung out while assisting other members of the crew to put on their parachutes. Surviving the descent he then took part in the perimeter defences at Arnhem. On 13 November 1945 Flight Lieutenant David Samuel Anthony Lord DFC was awarded a posthumous Victoria Cross.

FIGARO
THE CAT

During major servicing in winter 2002/3 AB910 was repainted to represent Mk Vb AB502 of No 244 Wing in Tunisia 1943 flown by Wing Commander Ian Richard Gleed DSO DFC. The son of a doctor, Ian Gleed was born in Finchley, North London on 3 July 1916. In 1935 he learned to fly privately at Hatfield before joining the RAF in March 1936 on a short service commission. Gleed's small stature soon earned him the nickname "The Widge". By the end of 1940, flying the Hurricane, he had destroyed nine German aircraft, probably destroyed three others and had been awarded half shares in two other victories. Late in December 1940 Gleed assumed command of 87 Squadron and by the end of 1941 he added to his rising score. In November Gleed was promoted Wing Commander and he now led the Ibsley Wing. More victories for Gleed followed in 1942 when he flew the Spitfire V on operations and his score rose to 12 and 3 shared

destroyed. In May Gleed was awarded the DSO and in July he was posted to HQ Fighter Command as Wing Commander Tactics. In December he became Wing Commander Operations and in January 1943 was posted to HQ Middle East where he was attached briefly to 145 Squadron for experience of operations in North Africa.

At the end of January 1943 Gleed became Wing Leader, 224 Wing. Early in March 1943 Spitfire Vb (Mod) IR-G AB502, was delivered to the RAF in January 1942 and shipped to Takoradi where, upon its arrival in May, and fitted with an Aboukir filter, it became Gleed's personal aircraft. The side of the fuselage below the cockpit now bore the same 'Figaro the Cat' cartoon that he had carried on his Hurricanes and Spitfires in England. Gleed flew AB502 on at least 35 operations over Tunisia during which he destroyed a Bf 109G near Medenine on 17 March to take his score to 13 confirmed aerial victories and 4 and 3

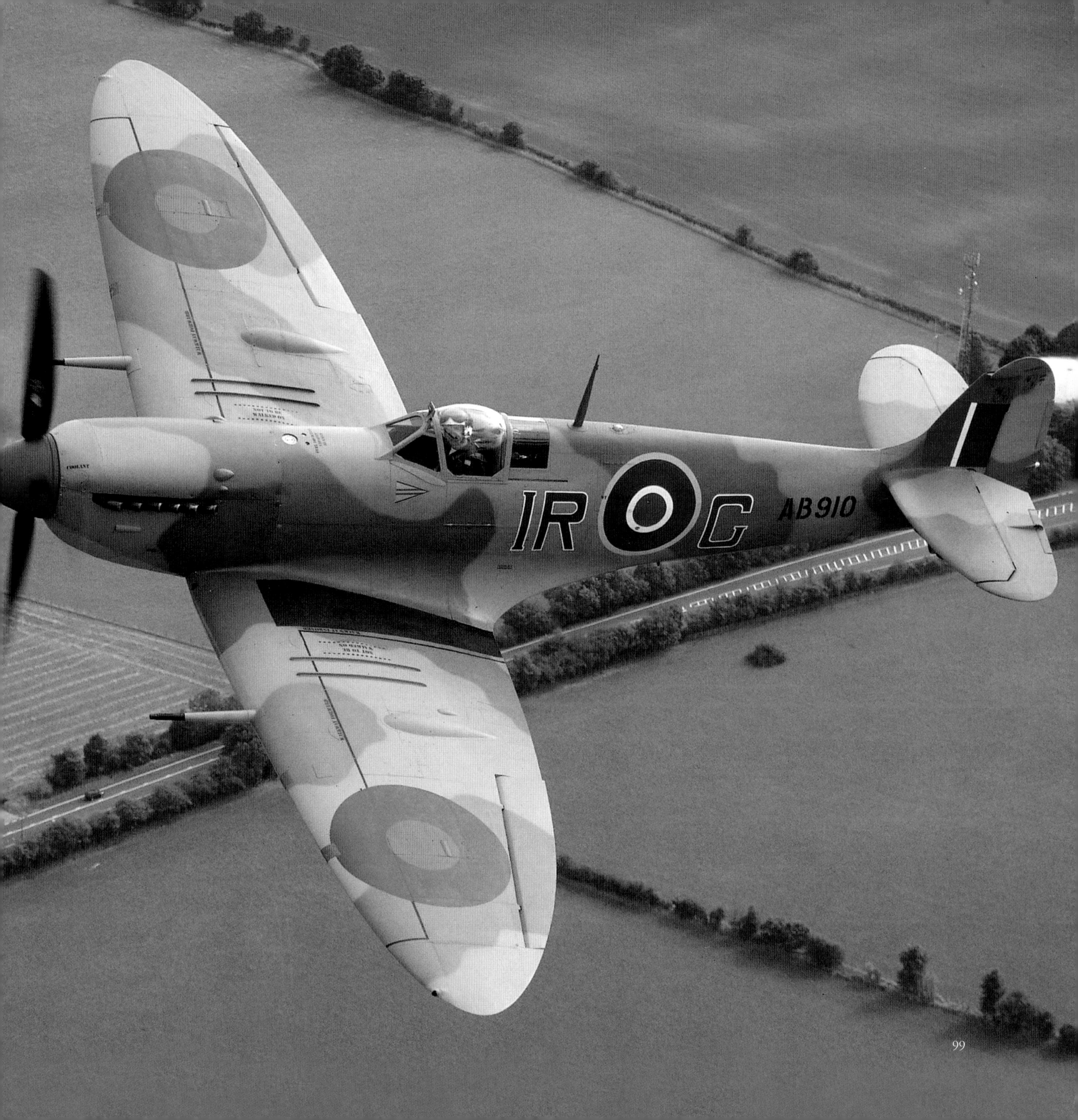
IR
C
AB910

shared probables. Flying the same machine he and damaged a Bf 109G in southern Tunisia on 7 March and near Cekhira a Bf 109F was claimed as 'damaged' on 6 April. On 16 April ten Spitfire Mk Vs and IXs of 145 Squadron led by Gleed took off on an offensive sweep over the Cap Bon area. Gleed's intention was to intercept the German *Freie Jagd* (standing fighter patrol) protecting the fleets of Italian Savoia SM 82 transport aircraft en route from Sciacca to Tunis. 145 Squadron destroyed two of the transports and three Bf 109s while a Fw 190A was claimed as a 'probable'. In all seven SM 82s were lost, four crashing and three force-landing in the sea. The RAF pilots got back to find that they had lost Ian Gleed. It seems likely that one of the German *experten* shot down Gleed. AB502 crashed on the Tunisian coast and was later found. Gleed was buried at Tazoghrane and his remains were later reburied in an Allied cemetery at Enfidaville.

"It was quite something to have our own plane, another milestone in our air force career. The ground crew was very proud of their plane and the number of trips completed. This showed good maintenance and a lot of luck. We hoped that the luck had not all been used up as it was usually considered that to survive a tour required about 70% luck and 30% skill. By this time Mickey was nearly worn out. The four engines were close to the hours for a complete change, the controls were sloppy, and she had dozens of patches on wings and fuselage. She took a lot of runway to get off the ground with a full load of fuel and bombs. We were the new crew given the oldest Lanc on the squadron, but we were proud of her."

MICKEY THE MOOCHER

My crew and I arrived on 61 Squadron, Skellingthorpe on the morning of 27 September 1944. During the next ten days or so we carried out our first two operations, one to Wilhelmshaven, on 5 October and one to Bremen on 6 October. We were then allocated a permanent aircraft, EE176/QR-M, with the nose art of MICKEY THE MOOCHER. It was a real veteran with 119 trips on the nose. [EE176 had previously been on 97 Squadron and it joined 61 Squadron on 20 September 1944. An aircraft lettered 'M' usually was known as *M-Mike* or *M-Mother* but EE176's nose received a Walt Disney cartoon of Mickey Mouse, walking towards a sign-post upon which was written 3 REICH and BERLIN, pulling a bomb-trolley on which sat a bomb. The Lanc became MICKEY THE MOOCHER, a name derived from Cab Calloway's popular slow blues song, 'Minnie the Moocher']. It was quite something to have our own plane, another milestone in our air force career. The ground crew was very proud of their plane and the number of trips completed. This showed good maintenance and a lot of luck. We hoped that the luck had not all been used up as it was usually considered that to survive a tour required about 70% luck and 30% skill. By this time Mickey was nearly worn out. The four engines were close to the hours for a complete change, the controls were sloppy, and she had dozens of patches on wings and fuselage. She took a lot of runway to get off the ground with a full load of fuel and bombs. We were the new crew given the oldest Lanc on the squadron, but we were proud of her.

She took us on our first trip on 11 October, a daylight one to the Dutch coast, with a fighter escort to bomb sea walls (dykes) in an attempt to flood German artillery batteries that were holing up the advance of the British ground forces. The raid was not successful although we bombed from low level. At this stage I could sense through Mickey, the feelings of all the crews that had survived over 100 trips in this special aircraft, passing on their experience and good luck for a successful tour, a sort of feeling of comradeship and well-being, which is hard to describe. Mickey was something to look up to, a guiding star. I get a similar feeling now, when, as a bushwalking guide, I lead a group of walkers through our magnificent Karri forests.

Our next trip was a 7½-hour night flight to Brunswick with 233 Lancs and seven Mosquitoes. This was an area attack with Cookies and incendiaries. A large amount of damage was inflicted. This was also a milestone as it was my 21st birthday, 15 October, and we had our first fighter combat. This is recorded in the debriefing combat report as follows.

Nearing the target area the mid-upper gunner spotted a fighter approaching from the port quarter above. It then appeared to side-slip into position behind them, he ordered the pilot to corkscrew as he opened fire, while also giving the rear-gunner the fighter's position and who, upon seeing it too, also opened fire. The fighter dived quickly away; the mid-upper gunner giving it a final burst as it disappeared out of range.

The next trip was another night one, 7hrs to Nuremberg with 263 Lancs and seven Mosquitoes, again area bombing, with a large amount of casualties and damage inflicted. We were beginning to get a little confident now, with our navigator keeping us on time and track and hence in the middle of the stream, and our bomb-aimer directing the bombing run with precision, and we were obtaining good target photos. Our next trip was another daylight one to the Dutch coast to attack the same batteries as before, also unsuccessful.

Mickey took us for her last operation on 6/7 November to bomb the Mittelland Canal at Gravenhorst. The marking force had difficulty in finding the target due to low cloud. We were called down to bomb at low level and I recall selecting full flap and wheels down to enable us to lose height in time. We were one of the few Lancs that bombed before the Master Bomber abandoned the raid due to low cloud.

On 9 November 1944 we flew Mickey to Netheravon, 1½ hrs flight from Skellingthorpe. Mickey must have been retired from operations then, because along with a Halifax and a Stirling she was to be loaded with Red Cross parcels to ascertain the number that could be carried to relieve allied PoWs as they were released by the advancing British troops in Europe. Mickey remained there till 30 November,

when we travelled in a Lancaster piloted by F/L Greenfield to fly her back to Skellingthorpe. Some other crew must have flown her away to 1653 CU after this, as possibly we were on leave. We were allocated our new QR-M on 18 December. What a difference to fly. When doing our first air test with no bombs and limited fuel, I opened the throttle on take off and we were flung back in our seats. She behaved like a sports car. We had now completed 12 trips and flew the new Mickey (although no art was ever painted on the nose) to the end of our tour except for a few weeks in January and February when she was being repaired after getting shot up and having a dicey landing. I returned to Australia in July with the probability of starting a second tour as part of 'Tiger Force', the new name of No.5 Group, bombing Japan. The Atom Bomb prevented this.

Flying Officer Frank Mouritz RAAF, Lancaster III pilot,
MICKEY THE MOOCHER, 61 Squadron, 1944

PHANTOM OF THE RUHR

There have been, according to various tomes, 36 Lancasters that famously recorded 100 operations or more during their wartime careers. All except *Q-Queenie/S for Sugar*, which flew 137 operations and was the gate guardian at RAF Scampton from 1959 until 1972, when it was put on permanent display at the RAF Museum, Hendon, were unceremoniously reduced to scrap after the end of the war. To date three wartime centurions have been represented by the BBMF Lancaster: *Mike Squared*, which flew 140 ops, *Still Going Strong!* (whose rear fuselage is displayed at Newark Air Museum, Winthorpe) and MICKEY THE MOOCHER. In 2007 the BBMF Lancaster emerged from its winter major servicing wearing the dual markings of 100 and 550 Squadron's Lancaster III EE139 PHANTOM OF THE RUHR. The port side shows PHANTOM as it would have been at the end of its service life on 100 Squadron, with 30 operations recorded in two rows of 15 and 'HW-

R' on the fuselage. 'BQ-B', the letters of 550 Squadron are painted on the starboard side. As far as ops go, 'PHANTOM OF THE RUHR' completed 121 not out.

EE139 was built by A V Roe Ltd at their Newton Heath works in Manchester as part of a 1941 production order for 620 aircraft built as Mk I/III aircraft powered by Merlin 20 or 28 engines respectively. The new Lancaster was delivered to 'C' Flight in 100 Squadron of No 1 Group Bomber Command at RAF Waltham (Grimsby) on 31 May 1943. The aircraft received the squadron codes of HW and initially the individual letter '*A for Apple*' but in early July 1943 it became *R-Roger*. EE139 completed at least 29 sorties on 100 Squadron, which was to remain in continuous action at Waltham and finally Elsham Wolds, until the end of the war. The first of PHANTOM OF THE RUHR's 29 ops on 100 Squadron was flown on 11/12 June 1943 with Sergeant

(later Warrant Officer) Ronald J. Clark and his crew. This all-NCO crew had arrived at Waltham having 'crewed up' at HCU in the time-honoured fashion. Jim Siddell, the navigator was a strong-minded York-shireman and the only married man in the crew. Harold 'Ben' Bennett the flight engineer was from Preston and a Halton 'brat' who had joined the crew at HCU. Lishman 'Lish' Y. Easby, the wireless operator was from the North Riding and a former civil servant. Les 'Trigger' R. Simpson, a Londoner, was the 29-year-old mid-upper gunner. His fellow Londoner was Doug Wheeler, the bomb aimer. W. G. 'Geoff' Green from King's Lynn, Norfolk, was the rear gunner. The crew actually flew EE139 for the first time on 2 June 1943. Six more training flights on EE139 followed and they began to realise that the aircraft was 'theirs'.

The Battle of the Ruhr was in full flow and when the crew's names were posted at the bottom of the Battle Order for the first time on 11 June. Ron Clark's crew survived the full ferocity of the battle and three raids on Italian targets. Early in the bomber's career the crew discussed an identity for *R-Roger*. Inspiration was found from the film *Phantom of the Opera*, which was then showing in cinemas. Ron Clark felt that the Grand Operatic Teutonic sagas of the British and the Germans performed nightly over the Fatherland should have been accompanied by the music of Siegfried. Sergeant Harold "Ben" Bennett, the flight engineer suggested painting a ghoulish hooded skeleton figure casting bombs out of the night sky. The ex Halton apprentice might have been influenced by feelings of revenge from his time as a ground engineer in Fighter Command when he had suffered frequent bomb attacks. The name PHANTOM OF THE RUHR and the skeletal figure were adopted though afterwards Ron Clark felt that 'something a little less ghoulish would have been more appropriate.' In front of the 'Phantom' motif was the mustard-coloured circular gas detection patch, which appeared on aircraft of No 1 Group Bomber Command.

PHANTOM OF THE RUHR was destined to become one of the most famous Lancasters in Bomber Command and Ron Clark would fly the PHANTOM on 42 occasions, logging over 165 hours in the aircraft, 147 of these on night operations. He captained the aircraft on 24 of the 33 operations PHANTOM undertook with 100 Squadron. Of those 33 operations, only three were aborted and when PHANTOM left 100 Squadron in November 1943 it had 30 'ops' recorded in two rows on the side. Operational sorties were marked with yellow bombs while a red bomb signified a trip to the 'Big City' as the bomber crews referred to Berlin.

Ron Clark

All told, the PHANTOM set out for the *Reich* capital 15 times. An ice-cream cornet represented raids on Italian targets and Ron and his crew were responsible for two of the four cornets on PHANTOM.

It was on their last trip, on 23/24 September 1943, when 627 bombers set out to destroy the northern part of Mannheim, that Ron Clark and his crew came closest to disaster. They took off with the first wave arriving over the target on time. The weather was clear with the glow of the Rhine clearly visible. Commencing the bombing run at 21,000ft they were immediately caught by the master searchlight and quickly coned by up to 80 more. Clark put the bomber into a steep dive but the searchlights stayed with them and a flak shell hit the aircraft. One shell damaged the starboard elevator. Another shell, which went through the bomb bay and out through the top of the fuse-lage without exploding, narrowly missed 'Lish' Easby at his wireless. The shell severed the starboard aileron control causing the aircraft to go out of control. With the control column jammed hard over Clark and 'Ben' Bennett struggled to regain control as they plummeted earthwards. Sergeant Geoff Green was immobilised in his rear turret by the G-forces imposed by the gyrating aircraft and blinded by searchlights. He joked later that at least he had enough light to finish his crossword puzzle and when Lish yelled, "Corkscrew!" from the astrodome, the rear gunner thought it was drinks all round at last!'

Bomber Command Memorial Window, Lincoln Cathedral.

Clark and Bennett finally succeeded in recovering the aircraft at 13,000ft but, still held in searchlights, were attacked by a night fighter from astern, damaging the port wing trailing edge and flap. Another shell hit the starboard tail plane. Having just regained control, Clark could see streams of tracer flashing in front of him and knew that despite limited control and considerable damage to his aircraft he had no choice but to throw PHANTOM into another steep dive. He successfully avoided the fighter and recovered the aircraft again, this time at only 4,000ft but was still followed by the searchlights that now appeared to be almost 'horizontal' in their pursuit of the aircraft. The crew managed to clear the target area and jettison their bombs, but PHANTOM was vibrating violently with the port wing and the tail plane "flapping up and down". Despite operating under the most extreme conditions Ben Bennett determined that the severe vibration was due to the starboard aileron

trim tab still being connected. Armed with a penknife he delved into the control pedestal and somehow found the right trimming wires, cut them and the vibration stopped. Clark flew the crippled bomber home and landed at Waltham without flaps and only partial aileron control. For their actions that night, saving their aircraft and crew, Ron Clark and 'Ben' Bennett received the DFC and DFM respectively. In the hangar the tail fin from a 30lb incendiary bomb was found in the air intake of one of the engines, indicating that bombs from above had also hit the aircraft. Severe damage was found to the tail and rudder and at least 300 shrapnel holes counted in the aircraft.

Ron Clark and his crew flew a further five ops with 100 Squadron before being posted with 'C' Flight to form the nucleus of the new 625 Squadron at Kelstern. They flew one more op before being screened, split up and posted. All of them survived the war with the exception of

the navigator, Jim Siddell, who was killed over Holland in a Mosquito in 1944.

The PHANTOM flew three more operations with 100 Squadron after the op to Düsseldorf before being transferred to the newly formed 550 Squadron on 25 November and re-coded BQ *B-Baker*. On 22 June 1944 when Bomber Command attacked V-1 flying bomb sites in the Pas de Calais and Pilot Officer J. C. Hutcheson, a Scot from Troon, Ayrshire who had been a chemist before the war, took the controls of famous bomber for the first time. He and his crew flew the 'PHANTOM' on 29 trips, some more frightening than the others and Hutcheson had the honour of flying the PHANTOM on the daylight operation to Le Havre on 5 September when PHANTOM OF THE RUHR became the first 550 Squadron aircraft to complete 100 operations. Hutcheson's last op at the controls of the PHANTOM was on 23/24 September 1944 before he left to become an instructor with 17 OTU. Both he and the PHANTOM' received a DFC each, the latter's ribbon being painted to the right of the first row of bombs. By mid November the PHANTOM had completed eleven more operations, which took the famous bomber's tally to 120 operations.

Despite becoming 550 Squadron's longest serving Lancaster, the PHANTOM, like so many other famous aircraft, was unceremoniously scrapped in February 1946.

If in the future the BBMF decides to adopt another 'centurion' scheme for the Lancaster then there are still a few names left in the archives, political niceties and artwork considered risqué, not withstanding of course.

JB138 *Just Jane,* which completed 123 ops with 61 Squadron has the same name as that used by the Lincolnshire Aviation Heritage at East Kirkby for their Lancaster VII NX611, which is complete and is powered by four working Merlins but is sadly non flyable. Three Lancasters had each racked up more than 100 ops while on 100 Squadron. *Take It Easy* was lost on its 111th sortie on 5/6 January 1945, *N-Nan* flew at least 115 ops before it failed to return from a raid on Nuremberg on 16/17 March and *Able Mabel* completed its 127th raid on 25 April 1945. Apart from the other others already mentioned, there is *The Saint* (119 ops), *Spirit of Russia* (109), *Flying Kiwi* (111), *Mike the Captain's Fancy* (101) and, appropriately, *Let's Have Another* (107). Why not?

ON THE FOUR WINDS OF WAR

A chill November wind swept across the desolate Norfolk airfield at Hethel near Norwich as the war's most illustrious group of Polish fighter pilots gathered to attend the official disbandment of 303 'Kosciuszko' Squadron. It was 27 November 1946 and many of those who had flown with the fighter unit over the past six years were present for what was described as the most painful day in the squadron's history. By the end of the war in Europe 303 Squadron had claims for 204 victories. But by late 1945 Polish military personnel in Britain had become something of a political embarrassment and HM Government shamefully wanted rid of them. The Poles had even been forbidden to take part in official victory parades for fear of upsetting the Soviet New

World Order and the Polish provisional government in Warsaw and the Soviet Union had refused to send delegations. It should be remembered that in September 1939 Britain had declared war after Germany refused to remove its forces from Poland, but that now was becoming, at best, a dim memory.

On 18 September 1946, three days after Battle of Britain Day – which the Poles in no small measure had helped the RAF win - the 'Kosciuszko' Squadron flew together for the last time as a unit. They took off in their Mustang IVs from RAF Coltishall and roared overhead in tight formation. Air Marshal Sir James Robb told the Polish fighter pilots who paraded before him: "You are men of courage, truth, honour, and proven worth." He added that their exploits would live in "undying memory" and that Britain owed them a debt that it would 'never be able to repay". A few months later, at Hethel, in an impromptu speech, Zdislav Krasnodebski, the 'Kosciuszko' squadron's first wartime commander, declared. "Our wings are being taken away from us... but we remain united in the belief that there will come a day when our machines, bearing the silver scythes of Kosciuszko, will touch down in a free Warsaw".

Many of the pilots where in a dilemma about whether to return to their homeland or not. One who had decided was Squadron Leader Jan Eugenius Ludwik Zumbach, CO of the 'Kosciuszko' Squadron from May to December 1942, who had left England two weeks earlier. Immediately after the war there was much 'bickering, back-stabbing and animosity among the Poles' and "friendships and memories," Zumbach said, "were about to be scattered to the four winds." Though born in Ursynow, near Warsaw he was able to leave England on a Swiss passport because his father was the son of Polish-born Swiss parents and he was registered as a Swiss citizen. Even so, Zumbach was told that he had to vacate British territory within three days. After three nights of hard partying with old comrades, Zumbach turned in his revolver, parachute and other RAF-issue equipment and headed for Switzerland. He would eventually domicile in Paris and from there begin another series of adventures.

Zumbach's military flying career had begun in 1934, when, concealing his nationality he had joined the Polish Army, serving in the infantry before being accepted by the *Lotnictwo Woljskowe* in June 1936. Graduating from flying training in November 1938 he was posted to *III*

Eskadra Mysliwska. In the summer of 1939 the neophyte pilot suffered multiple fractures of the left leg in a flying accident and he was still convalescing when the German invasion began in September 1939. It was only with some difficulty that he was able to rejoin his unit just as evacuation to Rumania began and eventually, he made it to France via Bulgaria and the Mediterranean. In May 1940, passed fit to fly, he joined a small group of other Poles, which was formed into GCll/55 flying *Armée de l'Air* Morane-Saulnier MS.406 and Curtis Hawk 75 fighters. On 10 June several of the Polish pilots claimed a Bf 109 but they in turn were all shot down by other German fighters and Zumbach baled out. France was on the verge of defeat and after several attempts to get away by air, Zumbach managed to get aboard a ship bound for England on 18 June 1940. On 2 August he was posted to 303 'Warsaw-Kosciuszko' Squadron, which became fully operational on Hurricane Is by 24 August. 'Initially formed in the Polish Air Force in 1920 by American volunteers who came to fight in the war against Communist Russia, it had been re-formed under the joint command of Squadron Leaders Zdislav Krasnod bski and Ronald Gustave Kellett. The latter gentleman was a former stockbroker who had joined 600 Squadron, Auxiliary Air Force in 1933 before transferring to the RAF in March 1939.

The squadron's first victory was recorded on 30 August. By early October Kellett had scored five victories and he was awarded a DFC while 303 Squadron had become the most successful Hurricane equipped fighter squadron in the Battle with around 50 confirmed victories (303 Squadron was officially credited with 126 victories, but

"Our ground crews were bedding the Spitfires down for the night. Placing chocks under the wheels, tying on the cockpit covers and carrying out last minute tasks so that they would be ready at dawn. All except the crews of the two missing Spitfires who stood apart in a restless, disconsolate little group and who occasionally fell silent and strained their eyes to the east, as if, peering hard enough, they would see their two Spitfires swinging in to land."

Air Vice Marshal J.E. 'Johnnie' Johnson

historians now quote between 44 and 58 kills that can be verified. Few point out that the Polish squadrons were not committed to the Battle much before the end of August). A total of 154 Polish pilots served with Fighter Command during the Battle of Britain and no fewer than 30 had been killed by 30 October. Zumbach's contribution in the Battle of Britain was eight and one 'probable' victories, the first on 9 September and the last on 27 September. On Monday 9 September Zumbach shot down Bf 109E-4 flown by Oberleutnant Schulze-Blank, *Staffelkapitan*, 4/JG 53 near Hastings. Schulze-Blank was killed. On 11 October 303 Squadron was withdrawn to Leconfield in Yorkshire for defensive duties. In December Zumbach was awarded a *Virtuti Militari* (5th Class).

In January 1941 the Poles returned to Northolt to re-equip with Spitfire Is and they began offensive sweeps over France. In February Zumbach was awarded a Cross of Valour (with two Bars to this in August and November 1942). (The award of a DFC from the British followed in October 1941 with a Bar to this in November 1942). In March 1941 the Poles re-equipped with Spitfire Mk.IIAs and in May Mk.IIBs replaced these. On 9 May when 303 Squadron put up six Spitfires for an afternoon 'Sphere' patrol to reconnoitre the French coastline they were jumped over Calais by Bf 109s of III./JG 3. The aircraft flown by Pilot Officer Zumbach was badly damaged by Oberleutnant Stange and Zumbach turned for home but as he neared Dover, the engine burst into flames. He jettisoned the cockpit canopy and baled out as the fighter dived for the sea. Zumbach came down unhurt on the outskirts of Dover despite having had his hair parted by a bullet.

In July 1941 Zumbach scored his ninth victory with a Bf 109E over the Channel. 303 Squadron moved to Speke near Liverpool for a three-month respite defending Merseyside before returning south to Northolt again in October to resume offensive operations equipped with Spitfire Vbs. Flying AB976 on 13 October Zumbach destroyed a Bf 109F for his 10th victory of the war. He also put in a claim for damaging a 'single radial-engined fighter' in combat. This was one of the first Fw 190s to be encountered and the German pilot probably should also have claimed a damaged, as Zumbach was slightly wounded during the dogfight. Another victory while flying AB976 followed on 24 October when he shot down a Bf 109E for his 11th kill. On 4 December Zumbach was posted to be an instructor at 58 OTU but by March 1942 he was posted back to 303 as a Flight Commander. Only two months later he was promoted to Squadron Leader and appointed to command the Squadron.

During Zumbach's period as squadron commander he flew three personal Spitfire Vbs, all of them coded RF-D and all adorned with a Donald Duck symbol in front of the cockpit on the port side. (The unit's insignia, which had been designed by one of the squadron's American founders - the circle with the US Stars and Bars and the Polish cap and scythes, was also added under the cockpit. His personal tally was marked by German crosses on the port side, 'confirmed' kills being outlined in white, 'probable' in red and 'damaged' without an outline). The first of these three Vbs was BM144, in which he claimed a 'probable' Fw 190 on 27 April. Zumbach's second specially painted Vb was EP594 (BM144 being re-coded as RF-H). In June, 303 Squadron moved to Kirton-in-Lindsey in Lincolnshire under 12 Group for a brief rest before being detached to Redhill for operations over Dieppe. Zumbach was flying EP594 on 19 August when 303 Squadron claimed five Fw 190s and one shared, two Ju 88s and two He 111s, for the loss of one pilot. Zumbach's personal contribution was a Fw 190, a Fw 190 'probable' and a third share in the destruction of a He 111.

That same day 133 (Eagle) Squadron pilot Flight Lieutenant Don Blakeslee, the renowned American ace and one of the outstanding pilots of WWII, was flying a Spitfire Vb on a sortie over Dieppe. His mount was EN951, which was destined to become Zumbach's third in the 'Donald' series. During its time on 133, EN951was flown on no less than 27 operational sorties by Blakeslee. Blakeslee's first victory came on 22 November 1941 when he shot down a Bf 109E flying a 401 Squadron Spitfire Vb. Now with 133 Squadron his second confirmed victory and first flying EN951 was on 18 August 1942 when he shot a Fw 190 down over France. Over Dieppe on 19 August 1942 and flying EN951 again, Blakeslee was credited with the destruction of a Do 217, one Fw 190 'probably destroyed' and two Fw 190s 'damaged'. (AB910, which the BBMF flies, was credited with one confirmed and one probable Do 217 over Dieppe). These were the last victories scored by Blakeslee flying with the RAF for on 29 September 1942 he and the other 133 Squadron American pilots were transferred to the USAAF. By the war's end Blakeslee had 14½ confirmed victories, three 'probables' and 11 'damaged'.

On 12 September 1942, a month after Zumbach had flown EP594 over Dieppe,

the aircraft suffered a serious accident with the Polish Squadron Leader at the controls. (After repairs it was eventually returned to 303 Squadron in December 1943). In the meanwhile, his next mount became EN951. As the third 'Donald', the artwork was larger and more detailed than on the previous two aircraft. Zumbach continued to command 303 Squadron until December 1942 when he handed over to Squadron Leader Bienkowski before joining HQ, 9 Group, as Polish Liaison Officer. In April 1943 Zumbach was promoted to lead the 2nd Polish Air Wing (133 Wing) at Kirton-in-Lindsey and later he attended the Polish Staff College, before leading the Wing again, now at Coltishall, in early 1945. (EN951 continued to serve on 303 until being transferred to 315 Squadron in June 1943. EN951 then moved to 19 Squadron and no certain records exist after being damaged on 20 June 1943). While flying Mustang IIIs Zumbach claimed his last victory, a Fw190 'probable' during the *Market-Garden* operation at Arnhem on 25 September

1944. Having finished another flying tour, he was posted on 30 January 1945 to HQ, 84 Group, 2nd TAF, as an Operations officer. During this, his final, tour of the war, Zumbach occasionally 'borrowed' an aircraft to visit various units in the front line. It was on one such occasion that following a navigational error he ran out of fuel in an Auster and ended up coming down on the wrong side of the lines, spending the last month of the war as a PoW. His final wartime score was 12 and two shared victories with a further five probables and one damaged.

Post war Zumbach flew contraband around Southern Europe and the Middle East. In early 1962 he formed an air force for President Tshombe's breakaway state of Katanga in the Congo and flew mainly armed T-6 Harvards. He later dealt in second-hand light aircraft and in July 1967 flew for the Biafran government, operating B-26 Invader bombers against the invading Nigerians before returning to France, where he lived until his death in 1986.

"'Stand by,' came the order to them at 10.30am.
All climbed into their Spitfires, strapped themselves
in and donned their oxygen masks ready to start up
the engines and get away. Soon after taking off to
guard a convoy in the Thames estuary, they were
cheered by the sight of about forty bombers flying in
groups of three spread out over a front about a mile
wide. Stephen, thinking the bombers had already
attacked the convoy and were retreating, was
surprised to find himself in the middle of them before
he knew it. 'The German aircraft were going round
in steep turns. Imagine them, forty very manoeu-
vrable and fast Messerschmitt 110 fighter-bombers.
We were chasing them and they were chasing us in
and out of the clouds. In a few minutes they started
to form one of their well-know defensive circles. By
this time several Germans were lying smashed up in
the water with the crews swimming round. The
Spitfires were now diving in and out of the circle
and never letting them complete it. I got my sights on
one bomber and gave him a long burst and one of my
tracer bullets must have hit his petrol tank, as in a
few seconds he went down flaming into the sea. I
climbed into the clouds just as another bomber
darted at me and we passed each other so closely that
I do not know how we avoided a smash. Turning on
his tail, I silenced his rear-gunner with a burst,
and as I closed the range the Messerschmitt rolled
over and fell upside down in the sea.'"

Flight Lieutenant Harbourne Mackay Stephen, 74
Squadron 11 August 1940. *So Few: The Immortal
Record of the Royal Air Force* by David Masters (1941)

123

'Kut' flew all his Night Intruder sorties in Hurricane IIc BE581 JX-E, which he christened NIGHT REAPER. In a brief 3-month period he cut down 15 enemy bombers over their own bases in France, including three Heinkel 111s in one night on 4/5 May and damaged a further five, and all this in only 15 night sorties.

NIGHT REAPER

O ver the winter of 2004/05 Hurricane IIc PZ865 emerged from a major servicing in a new colour scheme representing BE581 NIGHT REAPER, as flown by the Czech fighter ace, Flight Lieutenant Karel Miroslav Kuttelwascher during *Night Intruder* operations from Tangmere in 1942 with No.1(F) Squadron. Kuttelwascher joined the Czechoslovak Air Force in October 1934 at the age of 18 and clocked up 2,200 flying hours before the Germans occupied Czechoslovakia in 1939.

Three months later, he made a dangerous and daring escape into Poland by hiding in a coal train. From there he was able to make his way to France, where, flying Morane-Saulnier MS406 and Dewoitine D.520 fighter aircraft with the *Armée de l'Air,* he fought in the fierce but brief, Battle of France, claiming a number of German aircraft. When France fell, 'Kut' escaped to Britain via Algeria and Morocco and immediately joined the RAF.

On 3 October 1940 'Kut' joined No.1 Squadron and became one of the 87 Czechoslovaks to fly with the RAF during the Battle of Britain. 'Kut' or 'Old Kuttel' as his fellow pilots affectionately called him, served a full two years with 1 Squadron. During the early *Circus* operations in 1941 he shot down three Bf 109s and was credited with a 'probable. In July 1941 1 Squadron moved to Tangmere, 3 miles east of Chichester and it was from here that they commenced *Night Intruder* operations on 1 April 1942. The single seat Hurricane IIs were not equipped with AI radar equipment and the pilots flew long sorties of up to 3½ hours, with

long range drop tanks fitted, often in poor conditions and completely alone. 'Kut' flew all his *Night Intruder* sorties in Hurricane IIc BE581 JX-E, which he christened NIGHT REAPER. In a brief 3-month period he cut down 15 enemy bombers over their own bases in France, including three Heinkel 111s in one night on 4/5 May and damaged a further five, and all this in only 15 night sorties. 'Kut' also shot up several E-boats and steam locomotives on nights when he had ammunition to spare on the way home. He was awarded the DFC and bar.

Quite remarkably, the rest of the war was relatively uneventful for 'Kut'. While flying Mosquito night intruders he never even sighted another German aircraft. At the end of the war he returned briefly to Czechoslovakia but in November 1946, on the day that the communists effectively took control of his homeland, he flew back to Britain to rejoin his English wife and family. He joined British European Airways flying Vickers Vikings as a First Officer, and from 1951 as a Captain. 'Kut' died of a heart attack on 16 August 1959. He was only 42.

131

CITY OF LINCOLN

Lincoln became on of the top five aircraft manufacturing centres of the Great War with over 5,000 aircraft being constructed in the City's factories. Many of the Sopwith 806 types from Robey's Works flew to service from West Common, Ruston, Proctor & Co built BE2 biplanes and Sopwith 1½ Strutters. Clayton & Shuttleworth built more Sopwith types. After the end of the war in 1918, three out of the 37 military aerodromes that had been established in the County remained for the peacetime air force. As war loomed once again during the mid-1930s the RAF began a programme of expansion. Lincolnshire was an ideal launching platform for a possible bomber offensive. By the end of the war in 1945, 49 airfields in Lincolnshire were operational. Twenty-eight of these were bomber stations; more than any other county in Great Britain. Today, three of those military airfields remain active, at Waddington, Coningsby and at the RAF College, Cranwell. RAF Scampton, the home to 617 The Dam Busters, closed in

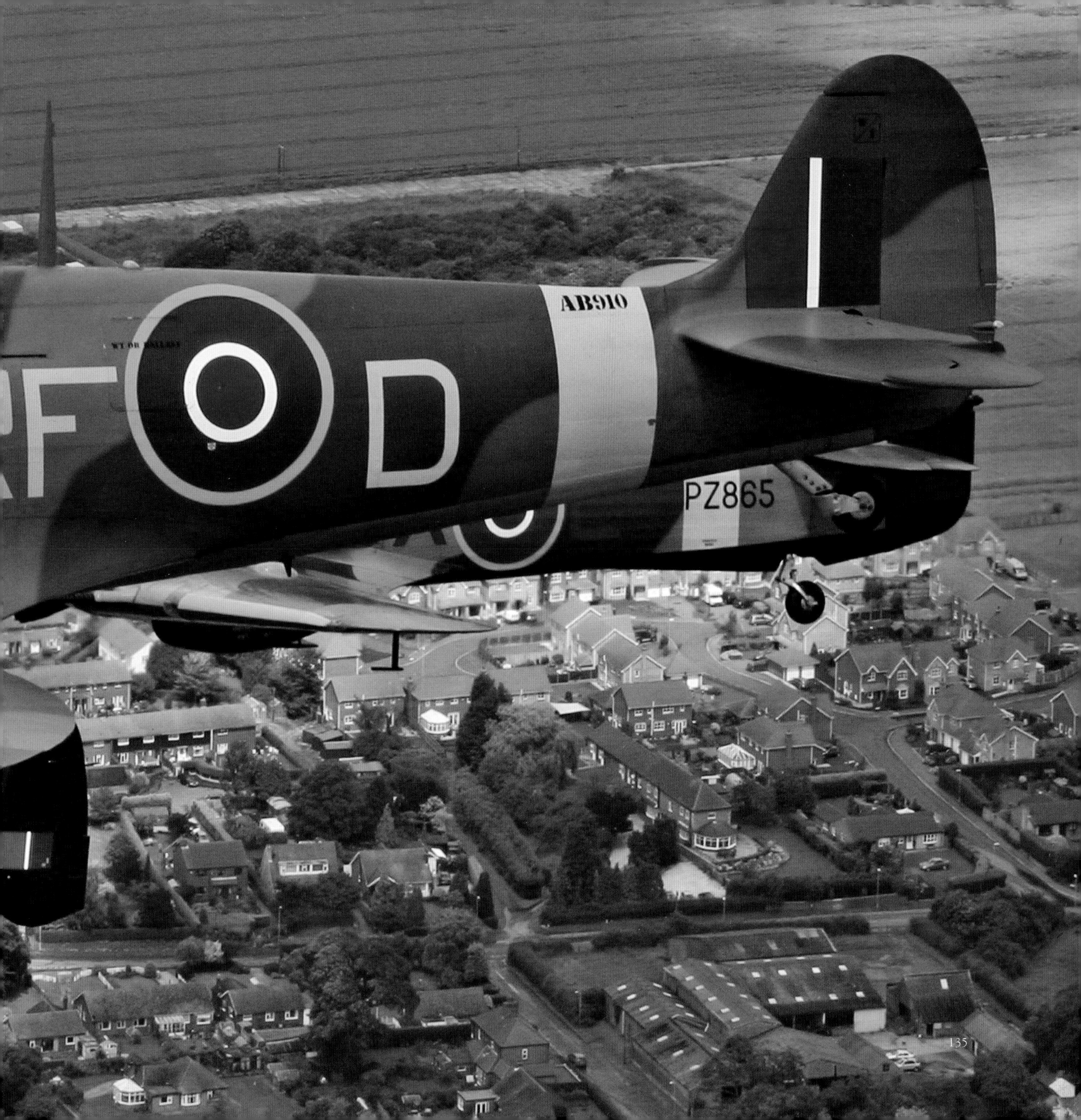
AB910
D
PZ865

1996. Since 1985 AWACs (Airborne Early Warning and Control Systems) Boeing E3D 'Sentry' AEW1s have been stationed at Waddington. Several of the BBMF pilots and crews are aircrew members on this aircraft.

The magnificent cathedral of Lincoln provided a distinguished landmark for crews during the war. The Cathedral probably never looked more poignant than on the night of 16/17 May 1943 when 617 Squadron's Lancasters set off from Scampton to attack the Ruhr Dams. Wing Commander Guy Gibson DSO* DFC* who led the attack, writing in *Enemy Coast Ahead,* said.

'The moon was full; everywhere its pleasant, watery haze spread over the peaceful English countryside, rendering it colourless. But there is not much colour in Lincolnshire, anyway. The city of Lincoln was silent -

that city which so many bomber boys know so well, a city full of homely people - people who have got so used to the Air Force that they have begun almost to forget them. Lincoln with its great cathedral sticking up on a hill, a landmark for miles around. Little villages in the flat Fenland slept peacefully. Here nice simple folk live in their bastions on the East Anglian coast. The last farmer had long since gone to bed; the fire in the village pub had died down to an ember; the bar, which a few hours ago was full of noisy chattering people, was silent. There were no enemy aircraft about and the scene was peaceful. In fact, this sort of scene might not have changed for a hundred years or so. But this night was different - at least different for 133 men: 133 young fliers and I was one of those men. This was the big thing. This was it.

'We were flying not very high, about 100 feet, and not very far apart.

I suppose to a layman it was a wonderful sight, these great powerful Lancasters in formation, flown by boys who knew their job. Below us, and also practically beside us, at 200 miles an hour flashed past trees, fields, church spires and England.

'We were off on a journey for which we had long waited, a journey that had been carefully planned, carefully trained for, a journey for which was going to do a lot of good if it succeeded; and everything had been worked out so that it should succeed. We were off to the Dams.'

The Airmen's Chapel in Lincoln Cathedral now houses the Memorial Books of 1 and 5 Groups, RAF Bomber Command. The books contain the names of 25,611 personnel who died flying from airfields in or near to Lincolnshire including 200 New Zealanders, 687 Polish airmen, 1,140 Australians and 1,233 Canadians. A service is held in their memory each Thursday at 10.30 am. Stained glass windows form the Bomber Command Memorial and the New Zealand Memorial. There are other memorials to units and individuals. A multitude of soldiers, sailors and airmen and WAAFs on leave and day's off frequented Lincoln's streets and watering holes like the famous 'Saracen's Head' better known as the 'Snake Pit'. It finally closed its doors in 1959. At The Lawn Visitor Centre in the former Lincoln Asylum, which opened in the 1829s and was used until the 1980s, is an exhibition dedicated to all those who served on Nos. 50 and 61 Squadrons in WW2. Original letters to serving airmen and women from family and friends are on display offering an emotional view of wartime Britain.

'STAPME' STAPLETON'S SPITFIRE FLIES AGAIN

During the 2006 season it was decided to temporarily alter Spitfire IIa P7350's XT-D codes to XT-W, the letters used when the 603 Squadron Spitfire was forced down over Hastings on 25 October 1940 with Pilot Officer Ludwig Martel at the controls. Martel received shrapnel wounds to his legs when a canon shell exploded in close proximity but he managed to land the aircraft back at Hornchurch and spent ten days in hospital recovering from his wounds. The repaired bullet holes can still be seen on the port wing. The aircraft letters were then changed to XT-L in honour of Pilot Officer (later Squadron Leader) Basil Gerald 'Stapme' Stapleton, who was born in Durban, South Africa on 12 May 1920 and whose nickname came from a phrase used in his favourite cartoon *'Just Jake'*. He travelled to England to take up a short service commission in the RAF in January 1939, being posted to 603 Squadron

in Scotland in October of that year. He was to see action with this unit first off the coast of Scotland and then over southeast England during summer and autumn 1940. On 3 July he and two other members of 'Green' Section shared in the destruction of a Ju 88A-2 of 8/KG 30 *Adler-Geschwader* over the sea near Montrose. On 20 July Stapleton, his closest friend, Flying Officer Robin Waterston, and Flight Lieutenant J.L.G. 'Laurie' Cunningham shared in the destruction of a Dornier Do 17P reconnaissance aircraft of *1 Staffel, AufklärungsGrüppe.120* off Peterhead. Leutnant Heuer and two of his crew were reported missing. 603 Squadron's Spitfire Is arrived at Hornchurch from Scotland on 27 August and they were in the action the very next day, losing three pilots killed.

Pilot Officer Donald K. MacDonald and

Laurie Cunningham died when they were bounced by 109s whilst still trying to gain a height advantage. MacDonald was on his first patrol and had just 15 hours on Spitfires while Laurie Cunningham was experienced with over 160 hours. On their last patrol of the day the squadron was bounced again and Pilot Officer Noel J. V. 'Broody' Benson, who had over 160 hours on type, was shot down after being bounced unseen. In an attempt to avoid this happening again, the CO, Squadron Leader 'Uncle' George Denholm, climbed the squadron on a reciprocal heading to that given by the controllers after take-off. Only when he believed that they had gained sufficient altitude did they turn towards the enemy.

On 29 August Stapleton was credited with two Bf 109E 'probables' at Deal and Manston and two days later he was awarded a third Bf 109E 'probable' north of Southend. On 31 August the death in combat of Robin Waterston, who was described as the Squadron's 'brightest character' was a great blow. While 603 were airborne RAF Hornchurch was attacked by fighter-bombers and three *Staffeln* of Ju 88s and Bf 110s, which dropped about thirty bombs on the station and at Biggin Hill. Four ground crew at Hornchurch were killed and two Spitfires were destroyed. Stapleton says. 'With no time to grieve we just got on with our job. We had to - we were fighting for our lives, our freedom and our country. Despite the casualties, I recall that we also had great fun. It was an exciting time and we lived life to the full. Each day was treated as if it were our last.'

On 3 September 'Stapme' Stapleton was credited with his first outright victory when he shot down a Dornier Do 17 15 miles southwest of Harwich. Stapleton's second victory followed on 5 September when

the Squadron lost 'a good friend and an excellent Flight Commander'. Flight Lieutenant Fred 'Rusty' Rushmer had refused 'Uncle' George Denholm's orders to rest and exhaustion was probably a contributing factor when he was shot down and killed in combat with 109s. Stapleton recalls.

'We had taken off from our forward base at Rochford when, at about 29,000 feet, we spotted a number of Dorniers below us escorted by 109s. I dived to attack the bombers but was engaged by a pair of Messerschmitts. I certainly hit one as I saw glycol streaming from the radiator but in my attempt to finish him off I was fired on by another German so I broke off my attack and continued my dive. In the heat of the battle I didn't see anything of Rusty but Bill 'Tannoy' Read later said he saw Rusty's Spitfire dive straight down vertically from altitude, through the bomber formation. He had obviously been hit. Rusty's grave in the churchyard at All Saints, Staplehurst, Kent, was only officially confirmed as being his in 1998 (marked 'Unknown' until then). That day I was reunited with a number of my former ground crew at the rededication ceremony. Rusty made the national news 58 years after his death.

'A short while later I managed to shoot down a Messerschmitt 109 which, unlike my first attack, was possible to confirm. During my dive from altitude I spotted a Spitfire at about 6,000ft diving vertically towards the ground, it's tail shot away. I then spotted a lone 109 in the same airspace as a RAF pilot descending by parachute. I latched onto the German and pursued him at low-level over the Kent countryside. As I fired short bursts he attempted to shake me off but I could see my tracer striking his aircraft and I closed in. I remember at one stage being

concerned that there was a village in my line of fire. He had nowhere to go but down and eventually force-landed in a field. I flew low over the site. The German was soon apprehended, initially by the unarmed cook from the local searchlight battery! A short time after the war I learned that the pilot was Oberleutnant Franz von Werra, his exploits made famous in the book and film, *'The One That Got Away'*, as the only German pilot to escape captivity (from Canada) during WWII and return to Germany. By all accounts he was an arrogant little man who was willing to lie to enhance his reputation. Well, he didn't get away from me!' Stapleton was also awarded a Bf 109E 'probable' in addition to the confirmed Bf 109 victory.

On 7 September Stapleton's Spitfire was hit in combat with 109s as he recalls. 'Having escaped the melée I managed to nurse my damaged aircraft back over the Channel, applying throttle intermittently so as not to overheat the engine, gradually losing height in the process. I eventually managed to force-land in a ploughed field adjacent to a hop garden. On climbing out of my aircraft I slid the canopy shut and turned to look for the nearest road. I spotted a couple having a picnic in the gateway to the field, their Austin Ruby saloon parked close-by. As I approached a sergeant-pilot who had landed by parachute joined me in a nearby orchard. The couple offered us a cup of tea and then a lift, not back to my aerodrome but to the nearest pub. What a contrast to fighting for our lives just a short time before!'

On 11 September Stapleton was credited with a Bf 110 'probable' and a Bf 109E 'damaged'. Four days later he scored his third victory when he destroyed a Do 17 and he was also awarded a Bf 109E 'damaged'. A

Bf 109E 'probable' followed on 17 September and on the 30th, he scored his fourth victory when he destroyed a Bf 109E. During October he again claimed a Bf 109E and he was credited with two Bf 109E 'probables'. The South African's sixth and final victory came on 11 November when he shot down a Bf 109E 20 miles northeast of Ramsgate. The award of a DFC was announced on 15 November.

'Stapme' Stapleton left 603 Squadron in April 1941 and served in various units, including flying 'Hurricats' with the MSFU, as a Flight Commander with 257 Squadron in February 1942 and as an instructor at Central Gunnery School. In August 1944 he took command of 247 (China-British) Squadron, flying Hawker Typhoons, receiving the Dutch Flying Cross for his part in the Arnhem operations. On 23 December 1944 as apart of a force of 16 Typhoons from 247 and 137 Squadrons at Eindhoven, he attacked a train, using rockets. One of his projectiles must have entered the firebox, as there was a terrific explosion and his radiator was punctured as he flew through the debris. Stapleton tried to nurse his Typhoon back at low level but he ran out of height and he force-landed two miles inside German lines near Mönchengladbach. He spent the rest of the war in

Stalag Luft I at Barth on the Baltic coast. Leaving the RAF in 1946, he flew for BOAC until late 1948, when he returned to South Africa. In 1994 he returned to the UK with his wife, Audrey to live at Ketton. One of only four surviving veterans of 603 (City of Edinburgh) Squadron who flew in the Battle of Britain and survived the remainder of WWII and the only one left who flew with 603 Squadron throughout the entire Battle, he was BBMF's most frequent veteran visitor. P7350 proudly wore the letters 'XT-L' until its repaint in 2009.

In 2007 Stapleton said, 'The BBMF and its hardworking personnel continue to preserve the memory of my long lost friends, an airborne memorial to the Few. I, for one, am well aware of just how much it means to them to represent such a prestigious organisation, which has rightly earned international acclaim and I wish them all the best for the future.'

Editor's note: *Sad to say, Squadron Leader Stapleton died on 13 April 2010 as this book was nearing completion.*